Speech communication

A BEHAVIORAL APPROACH

THE BOBBS-MERRILL SERIES IN *Speech Communication*

RUSSEL R. WINDES, *Editor*

Queens College of the City University of New York

GERALD R. MILLER

Michigan State University

Speech

communication

A BEHAVIORAL APPROACH

The Bobbs-Merrill Company, Inc.

A SUBSIDIARY OF HOWARD W. SAMS & CO., INC.
PUBLISHERS   INDIANAPOLIS   NEW YORK   KANSAS CITY

Editor's foreword

This basic volume of the Bobbs-Merrill Speech Communication Series sets the tone and establishes the point-of-view of the series: emphasis is placed on the socio-psychological nature of the speech act. Speech communication is viewed as a basic, complex behavioral process that exerts constant and pervasive impact on human existence and the progress of civilization. Underscored throughout this book, and the series as a whole, is the significance of speech as a tool used by man for understanding, manipulating, and controlling himself and his environment. The belief is stressed that the spoken word provides one of man's major means of maximizing the rewards and minimizing the punishments growing out of his environment.

Perhaps the major contribution of Professor Miller in this first volume is his analysis of the nature of models and of their role in the study of speech communication. A number of previous books have included models of speech communication, but there has seldom been a concerted attempt to discuss the purposes and limitations of such models. The present volume includes a discussion of the nature of models, a consideration of their functions in the study of communication, an examination of several models of utility to the student of speech communication, and a discussion of some of the potential shortcomings of communication models. As a result, the reader gains a basic grasp of this vital tool for the study of speech communication.

This volume also provides an extensive discussion of the implications of a process viewpoint for the study of speech. The material on purpose emphasizes the difficulty of assessing accurately the behavioral effects of any oral communication, a difficulty that arises from the interdependent relationships of the many variables, or factors, functioning to determine listener response. In this respect, the discussion of the essential prerequisites for process knowledge about speech communication is a feature not found in previous books.

Although attention is primarily focused on the behavioral dimension of speech, those ethical and aesthetic questions of interest to the student of speech communication—the value dimension—are not at all ignored. The writer places stress on the value implications inherent in any communicative act and develops briefly a viewpoint regarding the importance of values to the study and practice of speech.

Every effort has been devoted to providing in this first volume a sophisticated, yet readable, treatment of those matters deemed essential to an understanding of the speech communication process. **Speech Communication: A Behavioral Approach** is a volume the potential researcher and the practitioner of speech may both read with profit. Although the book is intended primarily for the beginning reader, portions of the manuscript will be of interest to more advanced students of speech communication. This book constitutes a genuine contribution to the literature of speech, a contribution of relevance to a diversified readership.

Russel R. Windes

Contents

Summary, 87

LIST OF FIGURES

Preface

A man's ideas and attitudes are products of many influences. For me, a primary collective influence has been the faculty and graduate students of the Department of Speech at the University of Iowa. It was in their midst that I first experienced the demands of rigorous scholarship and the joys of disciplined intellectual inquiry. Individually I have been affected immeasurably by the teaching and inspiration of Samuel Becker and Donald Bryant, men of different scholarly bents but with a common love for knowledge. To Milton Rosenbaum, who first introduced me to the mysteries of social psychology, and to my friends and colleagues at Michigan State University I owe an incalculable intellectual debt.

My thoughts have undergone continuous modification and change due to the prodding of numerous eager students. I thank them all for the insights they have provided. In particular, I wish to express my appreciation to Delmer Hilyard for a careful and critical reading of the entire manuscript.

My wife has always strenuously opposed any public pronouncements of gratitude. I therefore assert I am **not** going to thank her for patience, understanding, and sympathy. Because my children do not share this aversion to the public eye, I have no trepidation about thanking them for these same qualities.

G. R. M.

Speech communication

A BEHAVIORAL APPROACH

ONE

A general overview of the importance of speech communication

The study of human communication has a long and dignified history. With its roots firmly grounded in Greek and Roman antiquity, scholarly inquiry into the problems of effective oral communication still flourishes in contemporary society. Not only do traditional methods of investigating this distinctively human activity continue to thrive, innovation is the key word of the day; thus the anthropologist, the sociologist, the psychologist, the linguist, and the engineer—to name but a few—have developed new viewpoints on the process of speech communication. To say that intellectual ferment and intense activity have characterized the mid-twentieth-century study of speech would certainly not be an overstatement.

There are, of course, numerous reasons for man's persistent interest in speech, the process that he employs to carry on most of his daily transactions with others. Some writers have suggested that language behavior is itself intrinsically fascinating. The pioneering linguist, Benjamin L. Whorf, underscores this view, stating that there is a natural human tendency "to find language, mysterious as it is, the most fascinating of subjects—one about which men love to talk

1

and speculate unscientifically, to discuss endlessly the meaning of words, or the odd speech of the man from Boston as it appears to the man of Oshkosh, or vice versa."[1] Others have stressed that the gifts of language and speech are the factors that best distinguish man from lower animal forms, a fact that should explain man's desire to arrive at a fuller understanding of these phenomena. And the centrality of speech communication is further emphasized by the assertion—almost a modern commonplace—that human beings engage in a great deal of oral discourse. Quantitatively, speech communication comprises a major segment of our daily lives; in fact, so much "talk" goes on that a colleague has suggested—half jestingly and half seriously—that nothing is more socially overdue than a philosophy that stresses the virtues of silence. While this possibility may sometimes seem attractive, each of us realizes that speech is an essential dimension of the human experience.

Intrinsic interest, human distinctiveness, quantitative frequency— each of these considerations helps to explain our enduring concern with the process of speech communication. But the root assumption underlying this entire volume is that speech communication is, in addition, a crucial determinant of the extent to which we are capable of coping with the problems and frustrations that each day brings. More explicitly and formally, **speech communication is important because it is one of the primary tools that man employs to manipulate, to control, and to understand his environment. Further, for at least most individuals, skill in utilizing the spoken word provides one of the major means of maximizing the rewards obtained from the environment and of minimizing the punishments.**

Some discussion of certain implications inherent in this assumption will help the reader to understand my meaning. First, it should be emphasized that the terms "manipulate" and "control" are not used pejoratively. Of necessity, all behavioral activities, including speech communication, involve some degree of manipulation and control. The question is not whether one should engage in such activities; for from the day we enter the world until the day we depart, our survival is staked upon our ability to influence the events and objects that surround us. Rather, as you will see later, the cru-

[1]Benjamin L. Whorf, **Language, Thought, and Reality** (New York: The Technology Press of Massachusetts Institute of Technology and Wiley, 1956), p. 257.

cial questions concern the ends that manipulation should serve and the identification of those individuals who should exercise control.

Second, several comments about the terms "rewards" and "punishments" are appropriate; because, for many, these words have a crass, materialistic ring implying a marketplace view of man. As used in the above assumption, however, they encompass a much broader range of events. A reward may consist of an economic gain in a business transaction or a promotion at the office, but it may also involve some psychological state, such as the sense of good will that one experiences after contributing to a favorite charity or the feeling of contentment that accompanies the pleasure of a loved one. Likewise, while punishment may embrace such events as a summary dismissal from one's position or a blow from a police nightstick, it may also refer to a particular psychological state, such as a feeling of anxiety or of inadequacy. To be sure, the overt happening and the internal state will often be intimately related; e.g., a promotion will frequently carry with it the sense of having pleased a loved one, and a dismissal will almost certainly be accompanied by feelings of anxiety and inadequacy. The crucial point, however, is that the notions of "reward" and "punishment" carry with them no marketplace implications; men may derive rewards from pursuit of activities that are deemed to be of the highest purpose, and punishments may be much more subtle than the flagrant physical and economic abuses that we sometimes witness. A major goal of speech communication is to increase the frequency of the former, pleasant events, and to decrease the occurrence of the latter, unpleasant happenings.

At this stage, several examples will best serve to illustrate the relevance of the basic assumption stated above to those activities commonly viewed as speech communication behaviors. Consider the familiar situation of the political candidate striving to gain election to public office. In his campaigning, he attempts to structure his messages (here "messages" would be defined as the entire content of his campaign speeches) in a way calculated to elicit certain responses on the part of his receivers; in this case, the body of eligible voters. To put it differently, the candidate's communication behavior is used as a tool to manipulate certain environmental stimuli to which the voting public is exposed; and, hopefully, to exert some control over its potential response alternatives. To the extent that these attempts succeed, various rewards will be realized. The candidate will be elected to public office, with all of the attendant prestige and status that accompanies political power. He will be esteemed by his fellow politicians; they will regard him as a shrewd ally (or foe), who is not to be taken lightly. If the position won is at the intermediate echelons of government—say, state senator—and if the candidate aspires to higher office, his success in gaining election will increase the probability that he will continue to move up the rungs of the political ladder. Given that the candidate has a program of legislation that he strongly feels will benefit his constituents, his election assures an opportunity to champion vigorously the adoption of this legislation. Finally, his election to office reflects glory upon his friends and family. It carries with it the pleasant psychological feeling that he has enhanced the status of those whom he respects and loves.

On the other hand, the candidate's speaking may fall short of its mark, and he may be defeated by his opponent. Should this circumstance occur, he will suffer various punishments. For instance, conditions directly opposed to the rewarding situations mentioned above will prevail; his status and prestige will diminish, and he will feel anxious and inadequate, rather than pleased and secure. And whereas it is readily apparent that some of the potential rewards and punishments linked to this situation involve overt economic and social events, many other rewarding and punishing contingencies are linked to the candidate's own inner motivational states.

Some readers may feel that the above example is atypical. After all, how many of us ever become candidates for political office? But a moment's reflection will reveal that these same elements of manipulation, control, understanding, rewards, and punishments are present to some degree in every daily communication transaction. For instance, an analysis of my own purposes in writing this book and an examination of some of the groups of receivers for whom it is intended will further illustrate the relevance of the above elements to communication activities. Even though this volume represents an instance of written rather than spoken communication, it serves as a useful example for at least two reasons. First, it allows me to relate the situation to you, the reader, as a communication receiver. Second, although the book deals primarily with speech communication, excessive emphasis is often placed on artificial distinctions between communicating orally and communicating by means of the written word. As this example develops, it should become apparent that the two processes are quite similar, if not largely identical.

Consider a situation in which my professional colleagues are viewed as the intended receivers of my communication. In this case, the skill with which I manipulate the verbal stimuli appearing in this book will determine the probable responses of these receivers. If I am successful, many of the rewards derived from my communication with my colleagues will be psychological: an increase in my perceived competence on the part of a professional associate whose opinion I value highly, a complimentary book review in a professional journal, or the praise that I receive from colleagues at a professional convention. These rewards are inextricably bound up with the marketplace benefits; e.g., if my colleagues react positively to the book, many of them will adopt it for classroom use, thus increasing my financial gain. In addition, the expression of positive consensus among members of the professional community increases my chances for a desired salary raise, a promotion in professional rank, or both. Finally, reward may also be derived from the very opportunity afforded to present publicly a viewpoint regarding speech communication, to detail my own intellectual position to an audience of peers.

Now consider the interested student of speech, communication, or another relevant area as the intended receiver of my communication. In this context, the elements of manipulation, control, and understanding are readily apparent. It is my assumption that many of you are experiencing your initial encounter with a point of view concerning the functions and the values of speech communication. As a result, one of my major aims is to manipulate the word symbols appearing in this volume in a way calculated to ensure that each reader will gain a fuller understanding of the speech communication process. In addition, I am hopeful that exposure to my communication will assist each student receiver in the development of a set of beliefs, attitudes, and values about speech communication. Success in this undertaking will again gain me numerous psychological rewards. The student will regard me as a capable communication scholar, a title that any teacher dearly prizes. Hopefully, he will promulgate many of the ideas, attitudes, and values espoused in the book, thus ensuring that my particular viewpoint is socially supported by others in the society. Obviously, material rewards are closely related to these psychological outcomes; because, as was the case with professional colleagues, adverse reactions on the part of student receivers will lessen the probability of the book's use in the classroom. Thus, effective manipulation and control of the environment are once again largely dependent upon my skill in communicating with each student receiver.

It should be noted that the preceding example has by no means exhausted the categories of potential audiences, or receivers, who may read this book. Colleagues in other academic disciplines may peruse its contents; friends and relatives may be drawn to its pages; individuals employed in a wide range of vocational and professional activities may examine the book, on the chance that its chapters contain material of value to them. If my example were extended to include these diverse groups of receivers, the concepts of manipulation, control, understanding, rewards, and punishments would still be of crucial importance for analyzing the communicative act and for predicting the probable outcomes resulting from it.

This latter fact suggests an important consideration. The approach taken in the above examples implies that while the social context of speech communication may vary drastically, the basic psychological processes remain essentially the same. Or, stated facetiously, this book does not contain sections titled, "Speech Communication: A Behavioral Approach to Voters," "Speech Communication: A Behavioral Approach to Professional Colleagues," or "Speech Communication: A Behavioral Approach to Students"; rather, it is my position that an understanding of the factors common to **all** of these communicative acts is of primary significance. A discussion of situational differences that may result in varied communication effects in particular social surroundings will be found in other volumes of this series.[2]

The exclusively symbolic nature of many of the relationships discussed in the preceding examples merits emphasis. Often, the success or failure of a political candidate is entirely determined by his skill in manipulating the verbal environment to which eligible voters are exposed. By the same token, the image that many readers form of me will be based solely on impressions gained from exposure to the communication behaviors found in these pages. It is conceivable

[2]For instance, **Audience Analysis** and **Message Preparation: The Nature of Proof.**

that I could enhance this image and establish areas of control over these receivers' responses, **if** I were given the opportunity to interact intimately with them for a long period of time. But the important fact is that such an opportunity is not likely to present itself; in its absence, I must depend entirely upon written communication to manipulate and control these receivers, in order to maximize my obtained rewards. This same limitation frequently exists in speech communication. Although one may be physically present at a job interview or when delivering a speech to an unfamiliar audience, ability to use verbal symbols will determine the magnitude of the reward received.

Furthermore, as society becomes more complex, exclusively symbolic acts occur with greater frequency, and the number of individuals whose rewards and punishments are determined by ability to manipulate symbols becomes more numerous. While primitive tribesmen controlled much of their environment by producing and manipulating **things**—farm crops, sheep, animal hides—many members of modern, industrialized societies must stake a great deal of their success on skill at manipulating **words.** The successful advertising salesman, the widely read editorial journalist, the influential politician, the university valedictorian, even the couple who have achieved a happy marriage—these, and others, have been rewarded because of their word-symbol acumen. To repeat the basic assumption of this volume: all human beings use speech as a primary instrument for extracting rewards from the environment and for avoiding punishments.

The reader will have noticed that in all of the preceding examples the acquisition of reward by the message source is dependent upon his ability to elicit certain responses from his receivers. This focus upon behavior is maintained throughout much of this volume. In the chapters that follow, I have sought to develop a viewpoint that will increase the reader's understanding of the behavioral nature of both the speaking act and the outcomes accruing from it. My major objective is not to paint an oversimplified picture of this complex, psychological act, but rather to provide the reader with a flavor of its complexity, while at the same time establishing some analytic distinctions that will enable him to explain and to predict with greater accuracy the outcomes of a particular communication event.

But every communicative act, of necessity, involves a value dimension; it stems from certain ethical and/or aesthetic premises. Not only do we seek to understand how speech communication motivates men, we also reflect upon the question of whether it is **good** for them to behave as they do. Because of the centrality of these value questions, I have also briefly examined the ways in which they are related to the behavioral dimensions of speech communication. While this is not primarily a volume on ethical speech communication, I would have been remiss had I ignored the bond between values and behavior.[3]

[3]For a fuller discussion, consult another volume of this series, **Ethics of Speech Communication.**

Purpose and speech communication

The behavioral dimension of purpose

The preceding chapter has touched upon one broad dimension of purpose: the use of speech communication as a means of manipulating, controlling, and understanding one's environment. At this point, I shall examine one major purpose of speech communication within a more limited context.

Consider a simple instance of speech communication. You and I are seated together in my office, discussing a forthcoming university lecture series. The office door is open, and there is a good deal of noise coming from the hallway. I casually query, "Would you mind closing the office door? I'm having trouble hearing you."[1]

It is not difficult to identify the state of environmental affairs leading to my request. For me, the noise in the hallway is psychologically disturbing, and I wish to reduce it. My stated reason for the request is that the disturbance interferes with our ongoing communication; however, it is worth noting that a number of other motives may have impelled me to seek your assistance. It may be that I have a general

[1] B. F. Skinner has labeled a statement that takes this form a "mand." This label is derived from such words as "demand" and "command" and is used to designate a statement that specifies its own reinforcement. In this instance, the statement specifies door-closing behavior on your part as the necessary reinforcer. See B. F. Skinner, **Verbal Behavior**, "The Century Psychology Series" (New York: Appleton-Century-Crofts, 1957).

dislike for noise, that I hear the voice of someone whom I intensely dislike, or that I have a severe headache that is aggravated by the present situation. Whatever my motives, the success of my communication will be determined by the way you respond to the verbal stimulus, "Close the door."

Suppose you reply, "I'd be happy to," after which you rise, walk to the door, close it, and return to your seat. In terms of the behaviors in which you have engaged, my communication has been maximally effective. Not only have you demonstrated your willingness to engage in the physical effort required to shut the door, your accompanying verbal behavior also indicates to me you are pleased to do it. So I derive not only the reward of reduced hallway noise, I am left with the pleasant psychological feeling that you are an individual of good will, who professes pleasure in rendering this service for me.

The preceding analysis suggests that there are other possible behavioral consequences, each involving the same physical responses, that I would not perceive as equally rewarding. Thus, you might assert, "Oh, all right, if you insist, I'll do it." Even though you proceeded to rise from your chair and to shut the door, I would perceive that my communication was less than optimally effective. I would be concerned about the tone of your voice and about the indication, from the content of your response, that you were reluctant to comply with my request. This uneasiness on my part emphasizes an important consideration—that verbal behavior may itself acquire certain rewarding or punishing characteristics quite apart from other types of behaviors with which it is originally associated.[2] Thus, your oral communication would serve to indicate social disapproval of my request, and this disapproval would result in increased anxiety on my part regarding my original behavior.

Of course, you might also respond (although here the probability is low), "Close the door yourself. I'm too tired to get up." Given this response, my communication efforts have failed completely. Not only have you refused to perform the desired physical response of door-closing, both the tone and content of your verbal behavior indicate your lack of respect for me any your willingness to ignore my demands. Obviously, when faced with this response, I recognize a num-

---

[2]This phenomenon is linked to the psychological notion of secondary reinforcement. For a discussion of such learned sources of drive and reward see, for example, Judson Seise Brown, **The Motivation of Behavior,** "McGraw-Hill Series in Psychology" (New York: McGraw-Hill, 1961), pp. 138–194.

ber of available alternatives in the ongoing interaction. I may repeat my request, embellishing it with possible undesirable consequences (punishments) accruing to you as a result of failure to comply with my request. I may demonstrate feelings of incredulity: "Did I hear you correctly?" Or I may aggressively terminate the interaction: "Get out of my office! I don't care to visit with you any longer!" These alternatives are not, however, initially attractive consequents of my original communicative act; it would have been much more pleasing to me if you had honored my request and had shut the door. Therefore, I would eventually have to admit that my speech communication had not accomplished my desired end; i.e., the behavioral effects were not the ones that I had sought.

This lengthy discussion demonstrates the many complexities involved in evaluating the behavioral effects of an oral communication. Furthermore, the situation considered is a relatively simple one. Suppose that instead of the interjection, "Would you mind closing the office door?" the analysis had focused on the conversation about the forthcoming university lecture series. Assume that I had embarked on this hypothetical conversation with the intent of persuading you to buy a ticket to the series, and that after we had discussed the benefits of the series for some time, you had remarked to me upon departing from my office, "That certainly sounds as if it would be a worthwhile series to attend."

In terms of your oral response, it might appear that my communication had accomplished its intended behavioral effect. But has it? Not if, as just stated, my purpose was to induce you to buy a ticket. You may profess great enthusiasm for, and support of, the lecture series and still be unwilling, for a variety of reasons, to go to the box office and lay down the five dollars necessary to purchase a lecture series ticket. If you do demonstrate such reluctance, I have succeeded in eliciting your verbal support, but I have been unable to induce you to perform the other responses upon which the total success of my communication hinges. Thus, it can be seen that verbal acquiescence is frequently a necessary, but seldom a sufficient condition to insure the performance of other behaviors sought by the communicator. Indeed, as we shall note later, this frequent lack of correspondence between verbal behaviors and other classes of behavior is one of the major problems facing researchers examining the effects of speech communication on opinions and attitudes. Because the measure of attitudes most frequently employed in these studies is based on verbal responses, it is difficult for the investigator to determine if more favorable verbal responses toward, say, minority groups indicate an increased probability of other favorable behaviors toward the actual persons comprising these minority groups.[3]

But to say that it is frequently difficult to gauge the total behavioral impact of an oral communication accurately is not to deny the earlier assertion that every communicative act must, of necessity, involve considerations of behavioral effect. On the contrary, many students of speech communication agree that the analysis of behavioral effect is of central significance. For instance, Aristotle, whose **Rhetoric** is still regarded as a classic and definitive treatment of a host of issues relating to oral discourse, defines rhetoric (here, the term "rhetoric" is considered to be synonymous with "speech communication," even though one could spend considerable time stipulating distinctions between the two terms) as "the faculty of observing in any given case the available means of persuasion."[4] This definition, along with other explicit statements contained in **The Rhetoric,** illustrates that Aristotle conceived of the purpose of rhetoric as persuasion, or intentional behavioral effect, and that he considered a good rhetorician (here, the term "good" is used in a factual sense denoting effectiveness or success, rather than in any value sense involving ethical desirability) to be one who is capable of identifying the available means by which persuasion may be accomplished. The definition of rhetoric that Aristotle stipulates focuses heavily upon the elements of manipulation and control mentioned before. A contemporary social scientist would probably assert that a person who wishes to use speech communication as an effective tool for persuasion must be capable of "identifying and manipulating those relevant variables likely to exercise an effect on audience response." This latter assertion, while more jargon-laden, is a close paraphrase of Aristotle's "observing in any given case the available means of persuasion." In short, there can be little doubt that Aris-

[3] Several studies have demonstrated the inconsistency between verbal expressions of an attitude and other kinds of attitudinal behaviors. For instance, LaPiere wrote hotel and restaurant owners to ask if they would accept Chinese guests. Almost all of the proprietors responded that they would not. Later, LaPiere traveled to these establishments with a Chinese friend and found that most of the owners showed no hesitancy in accepting the Chinese guest. See R. T. LaPiere, "Attitudes vs. Actions," **Social Forces,** XIII (1934), 230–237.
[4] Aristotle, **The Rhetoric** (trans. W. Rhys Roberts) I. 1, 1355b25.

totle regarded behavioral effect to be the essential determinant of purpose in speech communication.

One does not have to turn to the works of the ancients to discover this emphasis on behavioral response. Writing in 1960, Berlo states:

> **In short, we communicate to influence—to affect with intent.** In ana-lyzing communication, in trying to improve our communication ability, the first question we need to ask is, what did the communicator in-tend to have happen as a result of his message? What was he trying to accomplish in terms of influencing his environment? As a result of his communication, what did he want people to believe, to be able to do, to say? In psychological terms, what response was he trying to obtain?[5]

Berlo sees receiver response as central to the success or failure of the communicator, viewing behavioral effect as the criterion to be employed in specifying the purpose of the communicator.

It may seem obvious that speech communication is primarily used to affect the behavior of others. Why, then, has so much stress been placed upon this point?

We frequently forget to practice what we preach. Many of the con-cepts that seem most obvious to us when called to our attention are forgotten in the busy activities of everyday life. The general semanti-cist's dictum, "The word is not the thing," is hardly an earth-shaking revelation; few students are slow in grasping the intellectual nub of the notion. But these same students (and their instructor as well) frequently exit from the classroom and proceed to violate this dic-tum in their daily behaviors. By the same token, each of us often forgets that we communicate to influence others; that when we com-municate, as Berlo has stated, we are "in the people business."[6]

Message emphasis. Often, formal instruction in speech communi-cation contributes little to eliminating this confusion. Too frequently, such instruction is almost exclusively message-centered. The student is told to prepare a speech dealing with some current political or social problem. In order to prepare a good speech, he seeks infor-mation concerning the problem from numerous sources. He dutifully extracts quotations from these sources, because he has learned that

[5]David K. Berlo, **The Process of Communication** (New York: Holt, Rinehart and Winston, 1960), p. 12.
[6]David K. Berlo, "Communication Theory and Audiovisual Education," **Audio-visual Instruction** (June 1963), p. 374.

a good speech should be heavily documented with evidence. He frequently prepares an outline of the speech and submits it to his instructor for evaluation and comment. When the outline is returned to him, he discovers that he has violated certain rules regarding parallel structure, that the speech lacks adequate transitions, or that his purpose is not clearly stated or properly restricted. If his instructor has spent class time discussing audience analysis, the student may realize that some of these faults will influence the extent to which he may obtain the desired response from his audience. If not, he may be left with the impression that there is a set of prescriptive rules that governs the quality of a speech, rules that pertain primarily to the message itself. Indeed, his only meaningful audience now becomes the instructor, because it is within the latter's province to respond in a way calculated to reward or punish the student's communication behavior.

One should not debunk, or in any manner negate, the value of the type of training just described. Certainly, there are many objectives that any responsible teacher of speech communication wishes to accomplish, and a number of these goals exist entirely apart from considerations of behavioral effect. They relate to a set of values concerning the ways in which a responsible communicator **ought to** employ oral communication. An emphasis on message-oriented factors is not, in all instances, at odds with the goal of favorable audience response. With many audiences, a speech that is clearly organized, makes effective use of evidence, and has a clearly defined purpose will undoubtedly result in greater behavioral change consistent with the communicator's purpose than a speech lacking these qualities. Regardless of the means employed, however, the end of any communicative act is some sort of behavioral effect; and success in determining how this effect may best be achieved is contingent upon extensive analysis of the people for whom the communication is intended, rather than upon a great deal of attention to the message **per se.** In short, message construction is secondary to desired response.

It may seem that the types of effects that a communicator may seek to achieve should be specified more narrowly. In particular, many students have probably had previous experience with a category system that attempts to classify speech communication in terms of particular sets of ends: to inform, to convince, to persuade, to entertain. A discussion of the genesis of these distinctions will indicate why they have not as yet been introduced and will also illustrate their relationship to the viewpoint maintained throughout this volume.

Traditional classification systems. The roots of these distinctions are to be found in the school of faculty psychology, which flourished during the seventeenth and eighteenth centuries. The faculty psychologists held that individuals have minds that can be divided into relatively separate and discrete compartments. One such compartment, or faculty, is Reason, another Passion, another Will. In order to communicate with these compartments, it becomes necessary to specify the types of appeals appropriate for each, construct messages containing these types of appeals, and present the messages to the intended audience. Thus, if a communicator wished to rely upon the faculty of Reason, he constructed a speech based on logical, rational appeals (a speech the purpose of which was "to convince"). If his primary target was Passion, his speech emphasized nonrational, emotional considerations (in other words, it sought "to persuade").

Several criticisms can be leveled at this approach to the problem of purpose. First, the faculty psychologist's view of the mind is burdened by a potential reification fallacy; specifically, the mind is conceived of as a unique physical entity, a **thing** rather than a **construct.** Most contemporary philosophers and psychologists hold that "mind" is a construct. In other words, some physical entity labeled "mind" is never observed; rather, the construct "mind" is inferred from watching the ways in which people behave. When it is observed that people do choose intelligent alternatives, that they are capable of organizing disorganized material, and that they successfully master numerous, complex thought processes, the observer infers the existence of some unifying process, a process to which he assigns the shorthand label "mind." In this sense, the construct "mind" closely resembles such psychological constructs as "set" and "attitude"; i.e., although an "attitude" cannot be seen, a number of behaviors can be observed that provide evidence for the existence of a psychological process that can be subsumed under the heading of "attitude."

If the existence of an entity called "mind" is improbable and unverifiable, the behavioral justification for dividing this nonexistent entity into compartments is questionable. Furthermore, on empirical grounds, such a procedure seems unrealistic. Effective speech communication is dependent upon the subtle blending of logical and emotional appeals. How can a speaker hope "to inform" an audience unless he is capable of "convincing" this audience that the substance of the message is worth learning? What are the distinctions among "informative," "convincing," "persuasive," and "entertaining" language? How much of the impact of a logical and rational speech is due to an emotional component resulting from learning experiences that stress the value of being logical? In short, is it possible to draw clear behavioral distinctions among these various ends or purposes?

A modern classification system. Still, it may be argued that a classification system can be useful, even if its categories do not correspond to clearly specifiable behavioral differences. One contemporary group of psychological theorists has found it useful to distinguish between the cognitive and the affective dimensions of an attitude—a distinction that might, in fact, be loosely compared with the inform-persuade dichotomy discussed above.[7] They have arrived at some means for specifying behavioral, or operational, differences between these dimensions, but the major value of the distinction lies in their reduction of the gross construct "attitude" to more specific components. Would it not be useful to reduce the broad notion of behavioral effect to more limited categories, on the assumption that a set of labels for the various behaviors sought by a communicator might enable him to think more clearly about his ends?

It would; however, categories such as "informing," "convincing," and "persuading" are limited in their value. When these labels are employed, communication frequently becomes message-centered, rather than receiver- or audience-oriented. In order to discover whether the speech is appropriate, the communicator looks to the types of message appeals employed, when it would be more profitable to consider the probable effect of these appeals on audience behavior. As a consequence, a well-organized and clearly developed speech may often be delivered in a psychological vacuum.

Let us examine an alternative set of categories. It retains the advantages gained from abstraction and specificity, but it bears a closer

[7]See, for example, Milton J. Rosenberg, **et al., Attitude Organization and Change: An Analysis of Consistency Among Attitude Components** (New Haven: Yale University Press, 1960), pp. 1–65.

relationship to what is now known about the psychological process of speech communication. This system places relative emphasis upon audience response, rather than upon message characteristics.

The response repertory. As a beginning step, let us consider a construct labeled "response repertory." This construct, common to stimulus-response psychology, is defined as the sum total of behavioral responses available to an individual at a given time; i.e., all of the possible responses that a person is capable of performing under varying stimulus conditions. How the individual initially obtained these responses and how some of these responses are retained over extended periods of time are complex problems of great interest, the former usually studied by learning theorists and the latter by those concerned with the phenomenon of memory. Obviously, it is beyond the scope of this chapter to treat these problems in detail, but the unfolding of this alternative classificatory system will bring to light considerations of particular relevance to learning.

Given this notion of a response repertory, it can be seen, as emphasized earlier, that the general purpose of all speech communication is to alter or to modify the response repertories of listeners. In other words, the speaker hopes that his audience members will leave the communicative situation demonstrating a changed pattern of behaviors. Having previously established and discussed this general purpose, it is now necessary to examine more specifically the kinds of changes in response repertories that a speaker may wish to effect. These distinctions form the crux of the classificatory system proposed.

Changing the response repertory. For reasons of clarity, the classification proposed is summarized in the following table. The Class I speech replaces the "inform" category, while the Class II speech subsumes the categories of "convince" and "persuade." The labels "Class I" and "Class II" are assigned for shorthand purposes, and because their denotative characteristics insure against excess semantic muddying.

CLASSIFICATION OF SPEAKER PURPOSES

Class I: To affect the acquisition of nonevaluative responses by listeners.

Class II: (1) To affect the acquisition of new evaluative responses by listeners. (Foster an attitude)

(2) To affect a strengthening of existing evaluative responses. (Reinforce an attitude)

(3) To alter existing beliefs by affecting the acquisition of different evaluative responses. (Change an attitude)

The Class I speech places emphasis upon affecting audience behaviors that are essentially nonevaluative in nature; i.e., bringing about an expansion of listeners' response repertories through their assimilation and retention of new cognitive, or informational, responses. The speaker's purpose can be simply stated: Here is a group of listeners, each of whom now possesses a response repertory consisting of some finite number of behaviors. My purpose is to increase the number of behaviors available to them by providing them with nonevaluative responses that are not now present. How can I best insure the assimilation and retention of these responses?

Because emphasis is placed upon the audience, the "How?" question posed above becomes paramount. The communicator quickly realizes that it is not sufficient to parrot facts; he must also attend to the means by which individuals learn such facts. Once this realization is clearly established, concepts such as motivation and reward assume primary importance. The speaker must motivate the audience to attend, and he must attempt to demonstrate the potentially rewarding features of the information presented. No longer is it sufficient simply to state, say, the major functions of the United Nations Security Council. Rather, it is of primary importance to insure the acquisition and retention of this information by the audience, an objective that can be accomplished only by demonstrating the potential value of this information to the listeners. The importance placed on affecting listener behavior minimizes the possibility that the speaker will engage in a vacuum-like presentation; instead, the necessity of attending to his audience will be apparent to him.

In the Class II speech, the same psychological dynamics prevail, but with the addition of an evaluative response dimension. To return to the Security Council example, the Class I speech aims at altering listeners' response repertories by the addition to the general concept "United Nations Security Council" of such responses as: "To provide an instrument for the pacific settlement of disputes," and "To provide an agency for dealing with threats to the peace." In the Class II speech, the speaker attempts to induce the acquisition of an evaluative (i.e., "goodness or badness") response on the part of the listener. The type of response desired thus becomes the crucial factor in distinguishing the two categories.

Like the Class I distinction, the Class II category is superior to the "convince" and "persuade" classification because of its emphasis on affecting audience behavior. In addition, it provides further important distinctions concerning the nature of the behavioral changes desired, distinctions that are subsumed and lost under these latter headings. An examination of the added precision gained from the proposed classification should provide further evidence of its utility.

Using the system. The distinctions involved can best be established by means of a hypothetical example. Suppose that a student speaker chooses to give a speech opposing the practice of animal vivisection. Now assume that he is to deliver this same speech to three different audiences: an audience of fellow speech students, an audience of members of the Humane Society, and an audience of members of a medical research society. What can be said about the kinds of behavioral changes the speaker wishes to effect in these three different audiences?

Members of the student audience probably have limited response repertories for the concept "animal vivisection." A good number will be unfamiliar with the issue. The speaker's task is to induce the audience to accept a sufficient number of nonevaluative responses to form a concept of animal vivisection, and then to supply for the audience an evaluative, "badness" response to be incorporated as a dimension of the concept. Thus, the speaker is attempting to sow the seeds of an attitude, to instill an evaluative behavioral response where none previously existed. Although one exposure is usually insufficient to lay a firm attitudinal foundation, the speaker's efforts will be substantially aided by the audience's lack of highly structured response patterns concerning the problem.

When the scene shifts to the Humane Society, however, the nature of the communicative purpose is altered. Here, the speaker faces the relatively simple problem of reinforcing, or rewarding, attitudes that already exist in the response repertories of most audience members. Their evaluative responses need not be altered in kind, only in degree. It is possible that no addition in the available fund of behaviors will occur; rather, the communicative end is the extension of rewarding stimuli to the audience, an end calculated to increase the probability that they will retain their present store of evaluative responses. Unquestionably, this is the simplest task a speaker may face; the psychological dynamics are such that success can be assured even with a rather mediocre effort.

Conversely, however, the members of the medical research society present the speaker with his most formidable challenge. The behavioral changes desired are complex and difficult to achieve. The speaker must effect the extinction, or removal, of attitudinal responses already present in the response repertories of his listeners, attitudes that are extremely resistant to extinction because of an extended history of learning. Should the speaker succeed in this undertaking, he next faces the equally demanding task of gaining the acceptance of diametrically opposed attitudinal responses on the part of audience members. Metaphorically, the speaker must first "lift out" of the listeners' response repertories certain evaluative responses, and he must then "put into" the repertories conflicting evaluative responses. Such a situation requires that the speaker utilize every resource available to him; even then, the probability of noteworthy success is often doubtful.

From this brief analysis, it can be seen that there are diverse behavioral processes involved in varied attempts by a speaker to effect changes in the evaluative behaviors of listeners, differences that are obscured under the general labels "convince" and "persuade." By placing emphasis on the different kinds of behavior changes a speaker may wish to effect, the classification proposed eliminates this obscurity. In addition, it insures that the speaker must constantly come to grips with the "How?" question, a challenge calculated to lead him to a fuller understanding of the concept of purpose viewed as behavioral effect.

The value dimension of purpose

Thus far, discussion has focused upon intentionally affecting the behavior of listeners. There is, however, another important dimension of communicative purpose. In order to understand it, consider the following statements:

> "In a democratic society, the purpose of speech communication is to provide a free marketplace of ideas."

"Speech communication should function to insure social order and harmony."

"Speech communication ought to promote all that is noble and human in man and combat all that is base and ignoble."

Whereas each of these statements specifies a purpose for speech communication, it is apparent that these purposes cannot be readily reduced to a set of behavioral effects. What are the behaviors that correspond to the phrase, "all that is noble and human in man," or the actions that are to be viewed as synonymous with "all that is base and ignoble?" Obviously, these behaviors are not clearly spelled out. Furthermore, if one attempted to make them explicit—to list a set of corresponding actions—individuals would disagree vehemently on which actions should be included on the list. To use an extreme example, a member of the John Birch Society and a Maoist Communist could never reach accord on which behaviors exemplify that which is noble and human. For that matter, a physicist would be unlikely to agree in all cases with a scholar of classical literature. In short, the purposes articulated in these statements differ qualitatively from the behavioral dimension that we have already considered; specifically, these sentences reflect a set of value judgments concerning the ends that ought to be pursued by oral communicators, rather than a concern with a set of factual outcomes accruing from a particular communicative act.

Failure to distinguish between the behavioral and value dimensions of communicative purpose frequently results in verbal quibbles over trivial issues. For example, I might suggest that Alolf Hitler presented a number of "good" speeches. Stung by my apparent respect and admiration for this madman, you might respond that Hitler never gave a "good" speech in his life. Throughout the lively thirty-minute argument that ensues, neither of us is aware that we are using the term "good" in two different senses: I, in a factual sense denoting means-ends effectiveness; and you, within the context of an ethical judgment concerning the ends sought by the communicator. Thus, my concern is primarily with the behavioral dimension of purpose, whereas yours is with the value dimension. If we had stopped long enough to establish this fact, there would have been no basis for further disagreement.

The importance of this value dimension of purpose is reflected in the emphasis placed upon it by many noted scholars of speech communication. The Roman rhetorician, Quintilian, defined an ideal orator as "the good man, trained in speaking," a definition that places emphasis on the moral characteristics of both the speaker and the causes that he champions.[8] As one would expect, Saint Augustine places great emphasis on the ethical ends served by rhetoric.[9] And in his **Lectures on Rhetoric and Belles Lettres,** the English rhetorician, Hugh Blair, focuses on yet another component of the value dimension of purpose, the notion of taste, a concept that is, of course, closely linked with aesthetic considerations.[10] In a more complex sense, such modern scholars as Kenneth Burke[11] and the late Richard Weaver[12] have also provided stimulating discussions of the value dimension of rhetorical purpose.

Concern with the value dimension of communicative purpose is of crucial importance. Every instance of speech communication is laden with value implications, often in terms of the strategy, or means, employed in communicating, and always in terms of the ultimate value implications of the act. To illustrate, consider a hypothetical situation that, on the surface, seems devoid of ethical or aesthetic considerations.

Assume that we are observing a lecture section of a university course in introductory physics, in which the instructor is discussing Einstein's contributions to theoretical physics. During the course of his presentation, the instructor makes the following statement: "$E = mc^2$." In terms of the classification system outlined earlier, his behavioral purpose is to effect the acquisition of nonevaluative re-

[8]This concern with ethics is pervasive in all of Quintilian's writings. See Quintilian, **De institutione oratoria** (trans. H. E. Butler) I–XII.

[9]Saint Augustine, **De doctrina Christiana** (trans. Sister Thérése) IV.

[10]Hugh Blair, **Lectures on Rhetoric and Belles Lettres** (Pittsburgh: John I. Kay, 1829), pp. 16–27 **et passim.** See also John W. Bowers, "A Comparative Criticism of Hugh Blair's Essay on Taste," **Quarterly Journal of Speech,** XLVII (December 1961), 384–390.

[11]Daniel Fogarty has suggested that Burke "seems to have dedicated his work to the fashioning of peace" (p. 57). Fogarty's volume provides a summary of Burke's theory, with emphasis placed on the ethical dimension. For the interested reader, it also provides citations for Burke's own writings. See Daniel Fogarty, **Roots for a New Rhetoric,** "Teachers College Studies in Education" (New York: Bureau of Publications, Teachers College, Columbia University, 1959), pp. 56–88.

[12]See Richard M. Weaver, **The Ethics of Rhetoric** (Chicago: Henry Regnery Company, 1953), and Richard M. Weaver, "Language Is Sermonic" in **Dimensions of Rhetorical Scholarship,** ed. Roger Nebergall (Norman: The University of Oklahoma Press, 1963), pp. 49–63.

sponses not previously available in the response repertories of many of the students. But how do questions of value intrude on this rudimentary act of speech communication?

First, this communicative situation rests on the fundamental assumption that knowledge is good, that what is known should be imparted to others. Most of us would take this assumption for granted, but we should be aware that it stems from ethical judgments that are potentially controversial. Perhaps the world would be better if some knowledge were suppressed, if people were to remain ignorant of certain notions and ideas. After all, the ramifications of the statement "$E = mc^2$" extend far beyond the confines of the classroom; the existence of arsenals of nuclear weapons can be traced in part to practical application of the information contained in the statement. Would mankind's lot be better if such weapons did not exist? Did Einstein act irresponsibly when he communicated this information to others? Is our hypothetical physics instructor derogating his ethical responsibilities by aiding in the perpetuation of such knowledge? The answers to these questions, and to others like them, rest on numerous imponderables; even so, each question is closely related to the value dimension of purpose.

Not only is the instructor's statement based upon a fundamental assumption regarding the desirability of imparting knowledge, it also implies a preference as to which kinds of knowledge are significant and important. Once again, others might question the ethical desirability of this preference. Perhaps a "better" generation of men could be fostered if students were to study theology rather than science; or, to put it in a manner more consistent with one perennial academic controversy, if students were tc study **more** theology and **less** science. But, even granted that one purpose of speech communication is to foster a "better" generation of men, what is meant by the term "better"? Once more, this simple communicative act has suggested a host of questions that focus on value considerations and their relevance to purpose in speech communication.

Though somewhat obscure, there is also an aesthetic dimension to the assertion "$E = mc^2$." In uttering this statement, the instructor has employed a system of symbols not drawn from ordinary language; he has chosen instead the language of mathematics. To be sure, one of the major reasons for his decision is to be found in the greater efficiency that mathematics affords, in the fact that the language of

mathematics results in greater means-ends effectiveness. Many physicists and mathematicians would also argue, however, that the
language of mathematics is more aesthetically pleasing; that, indeed,
"Euclid alone has gazed on beauty bare." If one assumes that an
ultimate purpose of speech communication is to create opportunities
that allow individuals to have aesthetic experiences, then the question becomes to what extent mathematics, as opposed to other language systems, accomplishes this end.

Unquestionably, other value implications could be drawn from
our hypothetical situation, but the ones discussed should serve to
illustrate some characteristics of this dimension of purpose in speech
communication. Again, it should be emphasized that the situation
chosen deliberately encompasses a communicative act in which
value factors are not readily apparent. Suppose, instead, the situation
were to involve a doctor who knows that a patient is suffering from a
terminal illness and who must decide whether or not to reveal this
information to the patient. In this instance, the ethical considerations are more readily apparent. Not only must the doctor reflect
upon the ultimate outcomes of each alternative: to tell the patient
he will live, to tell him he will die, or to withhold the information
from him. He must also, if he chooses to lie or to suppress information, consider the ethical aspects of the means of communication
that he has selected. In other words, he must decide whether or not
certain outcomes justify the presentation of untruthful communication or the suppression of information. Again, it becomes impossible
to avoid questions associated with the value dimension of purpose.

Here, it should be pointed out that questions dealing with the
value dimension of purpose are often closely related to questions
concerning the probable behavioral effects. Someone may assert that
the mass media have abrogated their ethical and aesthetic responsibilities by barraging the American public with communications that
are in poor taste and that place excessive emphasis on violence and
crime. Immediately, questions will probably arise concerning the
behavioral effects of these communications. Do they lead to an increase in crime? Is it possible that such communications provide a
socially acceptable means for displacing aggression, thus resulting
in a decrease of violent acts? What, in fact, is the current level of
public taste, and to what extent can these aesthetic preferences be
changed by exposure to the media? These questions of behavioral

effect may aid in arriving at decisions regarding the value dimensions of purpose, but it should be stressed that the two areas may be argued separately; one may admit, for instance, that communications stressing violence result in a reduction of the crime rate but, at the same time, maintain that such communications are not ethically desirable, and that they serve ultimate ends that conflict with the best interests of society.

Obviously, we have only begun to consider the value dimension of communicative purpose. One point should be stressed. In order to satisfy the role of responsible oral communicator, it is not sufficient to ask only the question: What type of communication will achieve maximum behavioral effect consistent with my intent? Although this query is an important one, every communicative act also involves ethical and moral judgments, a value dimension of purpose. Thus, the communicator must not only ask, "Will this work?" He must also ask, "Should I use this strategy?" and "Are the ends served by this strategy ethically defensible?" The establishment of harmonious counterpoint among these three questions marks the distinction between a responsible and effective communicator and the demagogue or the tyrant.

The study of speech communication: scientific and humanistic viewpoints

The preceding discussion of the dimensions of purpose leads to a consideration of the ways in which speech communication may be studied. What types of questions may be asked by the student of speech communication, and how may these questions be answered most effectively? This section will provide some tentative answers to these queries. In particular, it will focus upon the various methods, or philosophies, of inquiry available to students of speech communication and discuss the type of question that each method may deal with most effectively. It seems fair to state that two strains of inquiry dominate the contemporary study of speech communication: the humanistic and the scientific. An abbreviated treatment of the two viewpoints must, in many respects, be oversimplified; however, the following discussion focuses upon some of the relevant differences between them.

The humanist views his major role as investigation of the impact that speech communication exerts on human ideas, values, and aspirations. Although he is usually not opposed to the scientific method, he most frequently employs historical, critical, and philosophical methods in his own study of speech communication. The humanist is not disinterested in observing events occurring in the world around him. He just does not stress such techniques as controlled observation of large groups of people, systematic manipulation of the environment, statistical analysis of data, and replication of obtained results—all techniques of central importance to scientific method. Instead, he generally relies upon introspection, intuition, and rational authority to gain insights about the communication process.

The scientific student of speech communication sees his primary task as the development of behavioral laws regarding the process. He seeks to discover a regularity in events that will enable him to make explanatory and predictive statements concerning those phenomena that are of importance to speech communication. That is, the task of the scientist is to arrive at statements concerning the ways in which specified objects (e.g., sources and receivers of communication) will behave or respond in specified communication environments.[13] In pursuing this objective, he relies upon the scientific method; unlike the humanist, he does stress such factors as controlled observation, manipulation, statistical analysis, and replication.

Both groups of scholars could complement each other in the search for new insights regarding the speech communication process. The existence of the two viewpoints, however, has led to confusion and has created a situation that fosters poor communication and a lack of mutual understanding. The lines of inquiry and the division of labor have become blurred; and, on a few occasions, recriminations have been hurled back and forth. On the one hand, the humanist may feel that the scientist is tinkering with tangential questions of little import to the understanding of speech communication; on the other, the scientist may accuse the humanist of operating in an intellectual never-never-land, where no "real" answers to questions are ever unearthed.

[13]This statement is used later in this volume as a definition for the term "law." Such a definition avoids the ambiguities and problems associated with the notion of cause. See Gustav Bergmann, **Philosophy of Science** (Madison: The University of Wisconsin Press, 1957), pp. 75–131.

Such confusion results from an inability, or an unwillingness, to distinguish among the types of questions that are relevant to speech communication, and from a failure to analyze the methods by which such questions may be answered most effectively. Specifically, the author believes that the scientific scholar should concern himself primarily with the factual questions of speech communication (the previously discussed behavioral dimension of purpose), and that the humanist should direct his attention to the value questions of the area (the previously discussed value dimension of purpose). An examination of the two types of questions should indicate the reasons for this line of demarcation.

Questions of fact. Consider the following illustrative questions of fact: Can audiences distinguish between a sincere and an insincere speaker? Is it most effective to put the strongest argument at the beginning or at the end of a message? Will intensely emotional language result in greater audience attitude change than language of moderate emotional intensity? These and many similar questions aim at the discovery of behavioral laws regarding speech communication; or, more popularly, they deal with the "how to do it most effectively" problem. If satisfactory answers are to be provided for these questions, a great many procedural and methodological problems must be surmounted. The researcher must specify a clear operational distinction between the sincere and the insincere speaker; that is, he must stipulate the operations, or means, employed to identify each kind of speaker. He must also develop a defensible and useful method for measuring audience attitude change, and he must devise procedures for distinguishing language of varied emotional intensity.[14] These are no small tasks.

But once these barriers—each of which is a fundamental aspect of scientific method—have been scaled, the method of scientific verification provides the best answers to these factual questions. Its superiority rests on several considerations, the first being the control exercised to prevent other factors from influencing the outcome. Hence, in testing the question concerning language intensity, the scientist will attempt to structure the environment in a way calculated to hold other relevant variables constant. As a result,

[14]The reader who is interested in seeing how one investigator handled the problem of language intensity should consult John W. Bowers, "Language Intensity, Social Introversion, and Attitude Change," **Speech Monographs,** XXX (November 1963), 345–353.

differences in attitude change between audiences exposed to the two levels of intensity can be attributed with high confidence to the language factor. By contrast, one could attempt to answer this question by directing his attention to a debate between two ancient Roman orators, one of whom used highly emotional language and the other of whom did not. It would be possible to examine the apparent outcomes of the debate, to attempt to determine which orator appeared to have exerted the greatest behavioral influence on the audience. Given that influence could be judged in an unequivocal way, with what assurance could the investigator say that language intensity was the crucial determinant? Instead, one or many other political, social, economic, or rhetorical circumstances may have led to the outcome: circumstances that are controlled in the scientific experiment but that cloud the outcome of the historical inquiry just described.

Control is not the sole reason why the scientific method provides the best answers to the communication scholar's questions of fact. If clearly and adequately described, research procedures are public and reproducible, providing other researchers with the opportunity to replicate studies that have contributed new information. The mathematical models underlying statistical analysis enable the scientist to state the level of confidence that he can ascribe to an obtained result. The methods used in defining concepts assure that they are rooted to actual behavior, rather than in a context composed only of other language symbols. These and other considerations contribute to the superiority of scientific research in dealing with the factual questions of speech communication.

Two notes of caution should be added. First, practical necessity will often force the communicator to make judgments about the probable behavioral effects of a particular communicative act on the basis of the best information available. It would be patently absurd to expect that a communicator could carry out a controlled investigation or experiment each time he seeks to exert behavioral influence on an audience. Even here, however, scientific inquiry can assist him by establishing behavioral generalizations to guide him in particular communicative decisions.[15] Thus, if the communicator knows that, in general, audiences respond more favorably to highly emotional

[15] In fact, as the reader is probably aware, the goal of any science is the development of such generalizations (general laws) from which may be deduced the outcome of particular events. This point is discussed more fully in Chapters 3 and 4.

language, and if he has analyzed his particular audience in order to determine that there are no unique characteristics that set it apart from other audiences, he will possess valuable information to guide him in his choice of language.

Second, it should be emphasized that one class of factual questions has been omitted from the preceding discussion. One might ask whether Lincoln or Douglas exerted greater effect on the audiences who attended their famous political debates. Although this question is factual, it would be impossible to investigate it scientifically, because it would be impossible to reproduce the conditions surrounding the debates. Here, the best available means of inquiry are the humanistic tools of historical method; but, as was readily apparent from the earlier example of the ancient Roman orators, the conclusions reached would remain tentative because of the uncontrolled nature of the situation studied.

Questions of value. Let us turn now to the second type of question that interests scholars of speech communication, the question of value. For these questions, scientific method does not claim to provide conclusive answers; in fact, it alone is inadequate for the task.

The limitations of scientific inquiry in the realm of value questions can best be illustrated by example. Suppose a well-conducted scientific experiment demonstrates that audiences cannot determine whether a speaker is sincere or not. Furthermore, assume that everyone is willing to agree on the conclusiveness and validity of this finding. Does it follow that they will all concur with the statement, "It is desirable for a communicator to publicly support a cause in which he does not believe"?

Obviously, no such agreement will occur; indeed, there is likely to be considerable controversy about the statement, controversy that stems from certain ethical premises regarding speech communication. Thus, it can be argued that even though an insincere speaker may be successful in his behavioral intent, the societal ends served by speech communication require that communicators possess a private commitment to the beliefs that they profess publicly. The entire issue is inextricably related to the value dimension of purpose discussed earlier.

Numerous ethical and aesthetic problems are of significance to students of speech communication. These problems involve questions of value. Although scientific inquiry may provide helpful information for probing these value problems, it is inadequate as a method for achieving satisfactory conclusions. It is in the arena of values that the humanistic methods of critical, historical, and philosophical inquiry are of primary value. The goal of humanistic investigation should be the establishment of an a priori meaning in questions involving the relationship of ethics and aesthetics to speech communication. By focusing primarily on value questions, the humanist can develop a systematic discipline dealing with considerations of "what ought to be" in the realm of speech communication.

The need for cooperation. So far, an attempt has been made to demonstrate that a clear analysis and separation of the questions most suited to scientific and to humanistic methods of inquiry would enable advocates of these two types of scholarship to complement each other in the quest for fuller understanding of the process of speech communication. One set of problems, however, requires close cooperation between scientist and humanist. Such problems involve situations in which **what is** conflicts with **what ought to be.** For example, if it is unethical for a communicator to advocate a cause in which he does not believe, but if he can do so without this unethical conduct being detected by an audience, then scientist and humanist alike should strive to develop methods and conditions that would make possible the detection, or the elimination, of such unethical communicative acts. Granted, such an undertaking is complex and difficult; nevertheless, it is not impossible. Certainly, if **what is** can be brought into closer harmony with **what ought to be,** the effort involved would be more than worthwhile for all students of speech communication.

Summary

In this chapter the behavioral dimension of communicative purpose has been discussed, and an alternative scheme proposed for classifying the responses that a speaker seeks to elicit, a scheme that places greater relative emphasis on audience behaviors than do the traditional inform-convince-persuade-entertain categories. The importance of ethical and aesthetic questions—the value dimension of purpose—has been stressed, with emphasis placed on the relationship between behavior and values. Finally, the distinction between the humanistic and scientific study of speech communication has been made by specifying the type of question with which each may deal most effectively.

THREE

Process and speech communication

In the preceding chapter, the phrase "process of speech communication" occurred frequently. What does it mean to say that speech communication should be viewed as a process? What are the implications of a process viewpoint for those interested in the study of speech communication? This chapter will deal with these questions.

The meaning of "process"

In its broadest sense, the term "process" refers to a way of perceiving and responding to the world in which we live; in this respect, it is what the philosopher would call a metaphysical concept, i.e., a concept relating to the fundamental nature of reality. The process view places emphasis on continuous change. As Berlo asserts, acceptance of a process viewpoint implies that "we view events and relationships as dynamic, on-going, ever-changing, continuous . . . a happening does not have **a** beginning, **an** end, a fixed sequence of events."[1] Thus, the notion of process implies a universe in constant flux; it denies the possibility of viewing events, objects, or acts as static entities that are fixed in time and space.

It should be stressed that this broad concept of process reflects

[1]David K. Berlo, **The Process of Communication** (New York: Holt, Rinehart and Winston, 1960), p. 24.

31

a statement of faith about the nature of the universe. In this respect, it is similar to such assumptions as the scientific credo that asserts that the future will resemble the past; both of these statements are, in principle, unverifiable. The individual who subscribes to a process view of the universe cannot provide others with the necessary proof to establish the unquestionable truth of his position. Rather, he must take the position that, in terms of the best available evidence and in light of his own philosophical leanings, a process viewpoint offers the best working hypothesis for carrying out his transactions with the world around him.

How can the process viewpoint be applied to speech communication? Assume that you are a member of the local school board and that a vote on a school-bond proposal is pending in your community. One evening you receive a call from the president of the board, who requests that you appear at a local P.T.A. meeting the next evening to give a speech supporting passage of the proposal. Next evening, you arrive as scheduled, present your speech, answer questions from the audience, and depart, believing that, as a result of your speech, more audience members will pull the "Yes" lever than would otherwise have done so.

The series of happenings just described could be analyzed in a fixed, static way. It could be said that the communicative act began when the president called you on the phone, or when you actually began speaking to the P.T.A. audience. Furthermore, the end of the act could be arbitrarily marked as your time of departure from the meeting. Within these time boundaries, it would be possible to stipulate relevant fixed elements of the act: a communicator, or source (in this instance, yourself) possessing certain attitudes, ideas, and traits; a message, composed of verbal and visual stimuli; and an audience of individuals, each of whom also possesses attitudes, ideas, and traits. Within this context, each element could be examined without reference to its effects on the others. For instance, the verbal elements of the message could be scrutinized without considering the decisions of the communicator that led to the selection of these particular stimuli, or without speculating about the probable effects of these stimuli on the particular audience members for whom they were intended.

Such an analysis is frequently conducted by students of speech communication. Indeed, it is almost demanded, because, as we will see later, it is always necessary to abstract elements from the entire process if they are to be discussed meaningfully. But, and this is the crucial consideration, a process viewpoint argues that such an approach, though admittedly necessary, provides an incomplete description of the event. For instance, is it intellectually defensible to establish an arbitrary beginning point for the communicative act discussed above? Could it not be argued that the event began with your conception by your parents? For that matter, did not the conception itself involve the transmission of certain genetic traits that contributed to the impact of your speech to the P.T.A.? What about all of the learning and conditioning experiences to which both you and your audience have been exposed, experiences that greatly influenced the development of events? Did not social, economic, and political antecedents emphasizing the need for educational changes contribute to this situation? By the same token, can the end of this particular communicative act be clearly identified? What are the many conceivable ultimate effects of your verbal interaction with these P.T.A. members? And, last of all, is it not true that both you and your audience members were constantly changing during the course of the interaction itself? In short, the process position holds that there is no way, other than by arbitrary agreement, in which boundaries can be fixed, and no method by which change can be arrested.

Another description of the notion of process may be of greater utility for the study of speech communication than the statement that events are to be viewed as dynamic, ongoing, and ever-changing. The essence of this description is captured in the following statement: **Process implies a continuous interaction of an indefinitely large number of variables with a concomitant, continuous change in the values taken by these variables.** In order to arrive at its relevance to speech communication, let us analyze this statement more fully and define some of its more important terms.

The meaning of "variable." The term "variable" was introduced earlier in the discussion of communicative purpose, but it would be well to define it explicitly at this time. It is a key term that will be used frequently throughout the remainder of this volume. For our purposes, a "variable" may be defined as **any phenomenon that may**

assume more than one value. From a process viewpoint, nearly every phenomenon can be treated as a variable, because the situation of interest may almost always be constructed in such a way as to allow the phenomenon to have more than a single value.

For example, consider the phenomenon of death. As frequently used in ordinary language, death would not be considered a variable. The assertion, "I will die some day," implies that death has only one value; in this context, "life" and "death" (or "alive" and "dead") might be considered two values of a variable labeled "state of organic tissue." One could, however, speak of death in a theological sense and construct a set of circumstances in which it would be useful to think of death as a variable. Theologically, the death of a wicked man assumes a much different value than does the death of an acknowledged saint. Or, for the physiologist, biochemist, or biophysicist, the notion of death as a state of organic tissue could also be viewed as a variable; e.g., the state of organic tissue fifteen minutes after an individual has been pronounced legally and medically dead is decidedly different from the state of that tissue three weeks following the pronouncement. From this discussion, it should be apparent that the definition of a variable is dependent upon the way in which the situation is constructed and upon the purposes of the individual who is charged with the labeling.

Because dead people do not produce oral messages, death does not seem to be a variable of much import to the process of speech communication. This assertion is itself something of an over-simplification; for instance, it is often argued that some ideas have a greater potential for effect because the source of the ideas is dead; in other words, death sometimes seems to confer greater wisdom upon the communicator.[2] Even so, it will be helpful to illustrate the concept of a variable with a notion more intimately related to speech communication.

Such a notion is source credibility, a variable to be considered in greater detail later in this volume. Briefly, the label "source credibility" refers to **the perceptions that an audience has of a communication source.** These perceptions relate to such attributes of the source as his competence, or expertise; his trustworthiness, or

[2]One reader of the manuscript suggested that this sentence be deleted because of its irrelevance to my purpose. I have chosen to leave the statement in the text because it is another illustration of the complexity associated with any analysis of these variables.

honesty; and his dynamism, or vigor.[3] Thus, if a source is perceived as very competent and very trustworthy, the source has **high** credibility (one value of the variable source credibility) for the particular audience, whereas if he is perceived as very incompetent and very untrustworthy, his credibility will be **low** (a second value of the variable). Although the example assigns only two values to the variable, it should be apparent that source credibility can take on many values; i.e., it can be viewed as a continuous variable, assuming values on a continuum from extremely high to extremely low. This point is emphasized because of its significance to the process view that the values of variables in a communication situation are continuously changing.

The meaning of "interaction." With this definition set down, let us return to the original statement regarding the implications of process and consider the assertion that a large number of variables interact continuously with each other. The term "interaction" may be defined in numerous ways. Here, however, it is used to refer to **the conjunctive relationships existing between two or more communication variables,** relationships that serve to determine the observed communication effects. In other words, the concept of interaction implies that the outcomes of a particular communicative act are not determined by differences in the value of a single variable, but are a result of a number of relevant variables that function jointly to produce the observed effects.

Again, consider an example. One might attempt to predict the outcomes of a particular communicative act by studying the single variable of source credibility; specifically, the researcher might predict that a highly credible source will exercise greater behavioral effect on an audience than will a low credible source. Such an approach has limited utility, because it grossly oversimplifies the situation, particularly if credibility is viewed as a unitary concept based on a single dimension, i.e., a single attribute. In such a case, the values of the variable might be established by viewing communicators with college degrees as highly credible sources and communicators with grade-school diplomas as sources of low credibility. Given this procedure, it would follow that communicators with college

[3]Factor analytic research by Berlo and Lemert has isolated these three attributes as independent dimensions of source credibility. See James B. Lemert, "Dimensions of Source Credibility," a paper presented to the Association for Education in Journalism, Lincoln, Nebraska, August 1963.

degrees should be more successful than grade-school graduates in their efforts to elicit favorable audience responses. This might sometimes be the case. It can be seen, however, that the values of the variable, "amount of source education" (here used as a functional method of defining source credibility), will interact with the values of the variable, "amount of receiver education," to influence audience perceptions of credibility. For instance, a communicator with a baccalaureate degree in physics, speaking on a physics-related problem (here, the probable interaction of the message content variable further confounds the example), will probably not be regarded initially as a highly credible source by an audience of theoretical physicists; on the other hand, a communicator with a grade-school diploma might be perceived as highly credible by an audience of culturally deprived individuals whose average educational level falls at second grade. This example provides a very rudimentary illustration of the importance of interaction among variables.

The problem is much more complex than the example indicates. Figure 1 attempts to capture the flavor of this complexity visually. For purposes of clarity, let us identify the variables Source Credibility and Behavioral Effect as first-order variables, with the arrow serving to indicate a posited relationship between them. The concentric circles represent differing values of the two variables. The smallest circles depict the lowest values (i.e., lowest source credibility and least intended behavioral effect) that these variables may take, whereas the largest represent the highest values. Obviously, only a few of the possible values are illustrated.

Second-order variables are represented by the eight circles linked to Source Credibility by means of dotted lines. Once again, only a few potential values are depicted, and these second-order variables are themselves but a sample of the possible factors that may interact to determine perceptions of credibility. The diagram is labeled so as to indicate that four of the eight second-order variables relate to attributes that the source brings with him to the communicative act (Exogenous Determinants of Credibility), while the remaining four are associated with certain features of the act itself (Endogenous Determinants of Credibility). Thus, a Nobel Prize in Physics is a potential determinant of credibility that the communicator brings to the situation, but the language decisions that he makes while speaking are a part of the act itself.

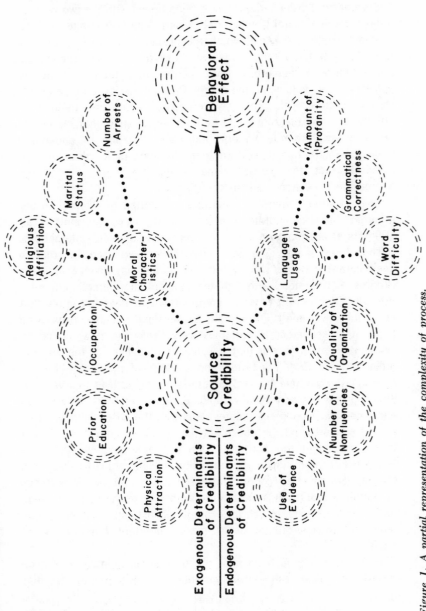

Figure 1. A partial representation of the complexity of process.

Several third-order variables have been linked with the two second-order variables, Moral Characteristics and Language Usage, in order to demonstrate the way in which the process continues to expand. Again, only a few of the values of these third-order variables are illustrated; also, numerous other factors undoubtedly interact to determine the values of the Moral Characteristics and Language Usage variables. This process of expansion could be extended infinitely; e.g., the diagram could be enlarged to show that the values taken by the third-order variable Religious Affiliation are dependent upon the interaction of still another syndrome of fourth-order variables. In fact, the general semanticist's "etc., etc., etc." could appropriately be appended to the diagram.

Some further comments regarding the notion of interaction are in order. First, commitment to the process viewpoint inhibits all attempts at adequate depiction of complexity of these interactions. Dashed lines, rather than solid ones, have been used, in order to demonstrate the ease with which boundaries may change for each variable. Furthermore, although the concept of interaction implies that all variables will function conjunctively, it does not imply that all of them will contribute equally to the final outcome. Thus, even if all other second-order variables were irrelevant, it would be an oversimplification to say that a value of plus five for the second-order variable Prior Education and a value of plus three for the second-order variable Moral Characteristics would lead to a value of plus four for the first-order variable Source Credibility. Some audience members may place greater weight on the latter ("I'll admit he is well educated, but he doesn't strike me as an honest man"). For those who adopt this attitude, such a simple additive procedure would result in an inaccurate prediction; in fact, students of speech communication often conduct research on the relative importance of certain variables in determining audience perceptions of credibility. Such research might, for example, investigate whether competence or trustworthiness is a more important determinant of credibility.[4]

In addition, although each of the third-order variables has been linked to a single second-order variable, it is obvious that they may

[4]At present, several of us are in the beginning stages of such a program of research; and, as the reader would probably expect, the question is exceedingly complex. A number of receiver and message variables will undoubtedly contribute to any conclusions that are drawn.

contribute to the values taken by more than one of these second-order factors. For instance, the third-order variable Amount of Profanity is linked to the second-order variable Language Usage; however, it probably contributes to the value taken by the second-order variable Moral Characteristics and, perhaps, to the value taken by the second-order variable Prior Education.

Finally, it should be stressed that the values taken by all variables determining source credibility are assigned by the audience members, the receivers of the communication. Their perceptions are paramount: in this respect, no communicator ever **possesses** source credibility; it is **conferred** upon him by his listeners. To be sure, it is assumed that certain objective characteristics, or attributes, of the source increase the probability that credibility will be conferred, but this assumption is dependent upon the attitudes and beliefs of audience members.

The preceding discussion is primarily intended to provide a feeling for the notion of interaction, but it has undoubtedly served to illustrate the extreme complexity of the concept of process. Even so, it can be argued that one might conceivably identify all the relevant variables and their interactions. If this were to happen, would it not then be possible to assert that the concept of process had been captured?

The meaning of "change." At this juncture, the idea of concomitant, continuous change—a third key notion in the statement concerning the implications of process—must be explored; for this idea further complicates matters. Not only are the variables continuously interacting, the values taken by these variables are constantly changing. This latter consideration further militates against a completely accurate description of the process.

Consider again the earlier example of your speech to the local P.T.A. urging passage of a school-bond proposal. Given the appropriate measuring instruments, your initial credibility for this particular audience could be determined; for that matter, it would be possible to measure the extent to which a number of the second-order variables listed in Figure 1 were contributing to the value of the credibility variable. But would the value of the credibility variable remain constant throughout your entire speech? Obviously not. Instead, factors associated with the communicative act (those factors labeled in Figure 1 as Endogenous Determinants of Credibility) would function in a way calculated to bring about changes in the value taken by the credibility variable. For some audience members, these endogenous determinants might lead to perceptions of higher source credibility (e.g., "His ideas make better sense than I thought they would," or "He certainly knows how to use language effectively"); whereas, for others, the value taken by the credibility variable might decrease (e.g., "He just doesn't look very trustworthy to me," or "That's the most stupid idea that I've ever heard"). In most cases, frequent fluctuations in value would probably occur (e.g., "I thought that first point was a good one, but this one certainly doesn't make much sense to me, " or "At the beginning, he seemed hesitant to look me in the eye, but now he seems direct and honest").

In short, the interaction of variables is not the only consideration involved in a process viewpoint; process also implies changes in the values of these variables. To be sure, the extent and rapidity of changes in the credibility variable will be partially dependent upon an audience's prior experience with a communicator. If, for example, an audience member has a rather firmly established perception of the source's credibility—as in the case of a noted political leader or a famous religious figure—changes resulting from endogenous determinants of credibility will probably be less marked than would be the case when perceptions of credibility are less firmly established; i.e., in a situation in which the source is initially a relatively unknown quantity. This is not to say, however, that relatively firmly established values will not change. For instance, some research demonstrates that if a highly credible source takes a position in favor of a policy to which an audience member is initially opposed, the audience member will subsequently report a somewhat less favorable attitude toward the source (i.e., there will be a reduction in the value of the credibility variable) and a somewhat more favorable attitude toward the issue.[5] Or, to look at the other side of the coin, it can be argued that every additional favorable experience that an audience member has with a highly credible source will result in a slight increase in the value of the variable.

[5]See, for example, Charles E. Osgood and Percy H. Tannenbaum, "The Principle of Congruity in the Prediction of Attitude Change," **Psychological Review,** LXII (January 1955), 42–55. Recently, several of us have incorporated the personality variable of Open- and Closed-Mindedness into incongruous communication situations. See Robert J. Mertz, Gerald R. Miller, and Lee Ballance, "Open- and Closed-Mindedness and Response to Incongruous Communications," Unpublished research report, Department of Communication, Michigan State University, 1965.

This analysis of the meaning of process could be extended further, but what has been said can be summarized as follows: First, the notion of process hinges on the two key concepts of interaction among variables and of changes in the values taken by these variables. Second, a process viewpoint stresses the extreme psychological complexity of speech communication; it asserts the near impossibility of capturing the full richness of this everyday activity in which each of us participates.

Implications of a process viewpoint

At the risk of appearing inconsistent, let us execute an about-face. The discussion of the meaning of process in the preceding section stressed the impossibility of capturing a process in its entirety. Even so, various philosophers of science have discussed the nature of process knowledge, and they have explicated the conditions essential to its achievement. This section will discuss these conditions and will consider their importance and relevance for the student of speech communication. At the conclusion of this discussion, the apparent inconsistency mentioned above should be largely resolved.

What would it mean to assert that we have process knowledge concerning one or more of the variables associated with speech communication, say, for instance, the previously discussed variable of source credibility? Speaking of the nature of process knowledge, Bergmann captures its essence as follows:

> . . . we know all the other [relevant] variables with which our variable interacts. . . . We know, in particular, how to compute the future as well as the past values of our variables from what we can now measure (provided we also know the past or future boundary conditions). Retrospectively we know, furthermore, what the present value of our variable would have been if some earlier state of the system had been different from what it actually was. **Prospectively, we know how to influence its (and the other relevant variables') future values by present interference with the system from outside; and we also know the limits of such interference** [boldface mine]. What else, I ask, could we possibly want to know about the variable in a scientific way?[6]

In other words, given a closed system of speech communication, process knowledge would enable us to compute the past and future

[6]Gustav Bergmann, **Philosophy of Science** (Madison: The University of Wisconsin Press, 1957), p. 100.

values of the credibility variable. Also, such knowledge would allow us to examine various states in which the system might be found, and to predict the present value of the credibility variable for each of these states. Finally, and of crucial significance, it would allow us to influence the future value of the credibility variable by outside interference with the system. That is, we would be able to predict with great precision changes in the value of credibility resulting from the outside manipulation of other relevant variables that interact with it. As communicators, each of us attempts to accomplish this latter objective in various crude ways, i.e., we endeavor to predict the ways in which we can increase our credibility by manipulating other variables that influence it. The acquisition of process knowledge would serve to perfect this endeavor, because it would enable us to make such predictions with complete accuracy.

Obviously, scientific study of speech communication has not as yet approached anything resembling process knowledge; however, such knowledge is, in principle, at least a possibility. Should communicators possess process knowledge, they would be assured of maximum predictability, as well as the opportunity to manipulate their environments through communication in a way calculated to bring about desired behavioral responses on the part of their receivers. Here, of course, some would raise ethical questions concerning the desirability of such a situation. They would argue that such knowledge reduces us to mere automatons, puppets dangling at the ends of scientific threads. Although an extensive analysis of this argument is beyond the scope of this section, it has already been pointed out that any communicative act involves some attempt at manipulation. Those who oppose any effort to acquire process knowledge regarding speech communication thus seem to argue that manipulation is acceptable as long as one does not become too good at it. Such a position largely negates the status of knowledge as a desirable value; i.e., it holds that ignorance is good, that in some areas it is not desirable to seek as much knowledge as it is possible to obtain. Of course, it can also be asserted that the acquisition of process knowledge regarding speech communication (or, for that matter, the achievement of any degree of understanding at all) is impossible. But the validity of this argument is best tested by continued research that aims at the development of a body of such knowledge. Finally, to endorse both of these arguments, as some have done, is logically inconsistent, because the first implies the possibility of extensive scientific knowledge regarding speech communication, and the second asserts that such knowledge is impossible.

Our primary concern here, however, is not with the ethical issues associated with the development of process knowledge, but rather with the conditions essential to its acquisition.[7] What are these conditions, and what are their implications for students of speech communication?

Acquisition of process knowledge. First, as indicated by several remarks in the preceding discussion, the acquisition of process knowledge requires closure of the system. To say that a system is closed implies that its boundaries are known and that it is possible to prevent the intrusion of other relevant variables into the system. Metaphorically, one might think of a communication situation that is psychologically "fenced off," and within which it is possible to stipulate the variables at work. Obviously, the addition of one unknown relevant variable (a breakdown in closure) will change the existing relationships and the values taken by the known variables.

A second prerequisite to process knowledge is alluded to in the immediately preceding statement: complete sets of relevant variables. For instance, to have process knowledge about the communication variable of source credibility, it would be necessary to know the complete set of relevant variables that interact to determine its value. It would, of course, be possible to establish a relatively closed system (the first prerequisite) without being able to stipulate all of the relevant variables at work within that system.

Finally, the term "relationships" has been used above. This term suggests the third condition essential to the acquisition of process knowledge: laws. Not only must it be possible to stipulate all relevant variables, the laws pertaining to these variables must be known. For our purposes, "laws" will be defined as **statements that describe the way a specified object will behave in a specified environment.** An example will illustrate the functioning of such a law.

Take as our objects the various audience members exposed to a communicator. Assume that we can specify all of the variables that influence their perceptions of a source's credibility, and that the system is closed to prevent the intrusion of new variables. For simplicity, grant that for each of these audience members the same

[7]Some of these ethical issues are discussed briefly in Chapter 5.

three variables function conjunctively to determine the value of the credibility variable. If we can state that a value of **x** for Variable 1, a value of **y** for Variable 2, and a value of **z** for Variable 3 will invariantly result in a value of **a** for the source credibility variable, then we know a law concerning communication; i.e., if $V^1 = $ **x**, $V^2 = $ **y**, and $V^3 = $ **z**; then SC = **a**. Or, stated in a manner consistent with the above definition of laws, if audience members (objects) are placed in a closed communication system (environment) which possesses qualities **x**, **y**, and **z** (specified values for the relevant variables which determine source credibility), then they will behave by assigning a value of **a** to the source's over-all credibility. Furthermore, the knowledge of one such law enables us to develop predictions about changes in the values of a particular variable that are attributable to changes in the values taken by other variables. In short, we not only know the relevant variables, we know the ways in which they interact.

Obviously, the three conditions essential to the acquisition of process knowledge concerning speech communication are closely related to each other. A breakdown in closure will result in the intrusion of another relevant variable into the system. This, in turn, means that we no longer know the complete set of relevant variables; consequently, if we wish to explain and predict communication behavior accurately, it becomes necessary to develop new laws. But given that all of these conditions are met, we can, as the earlier quotation by Bergmann suggests, know all that is scientifically important about the particular communication variable under investigation.

It may seem that this discussion has strayed afield from material appropriate to an introductory volume in speech communication. The matters that have been considered, however, are intimately related to the discussion of the importance of speech communication found in Chapter 1; i.e., they affect the extent to which speech communication can serve as a useful tool for manipulating, controlling, and understanding one's environment. Successful environmental manipulation through communication depends upon knowledge of the relevant variables; it also hinges upon an understanding of the ways in which these variables interact.

The necessity for closure. How does the requirement of a closed system affect the study of speech communication? In the typical, ongoing communication situation, closure is exceedingly difficult, if not impossible. For illustration, return to your hypothetical speech before an audience of P.T.A. members. Because you are a conscientious communicator, you try to analyze your audience carefully, to identify the variables that will influence their responses to your communication. In addition, you plan a message aimed at changing the values of those variables likely to produce negative responses and at reinforcing the values of those factors that will facilitate your desired behavioral outcome. All is proceeding smoothly, when suddenly, an audience member faints. Your speech is interrupted while the stricken individual is removed from the room. Once order is restored and you resume your presentation, you are aware that things are not going as smoothly as they were prior to the interruption. Indeed, this unexpected event produces such a disquieting effect that you depart for home with the feeling that you have been only minimally successful in accomplishing your purpose.

This example may seem far-fetched (after all, how many times do audience members faint during a speech?), but it illustrates the difficulty of maintaining a closed system in everyday communication activity. Given that the physical collapse of an audience member is a relevant variable affecting the responses of other audience members to your speech, all of your predictions must now be altered. To the extent that it is impossible to correct for the intrusion of this variable, your ability to manipulate and to control the environment is reduced. To be sure, if fainting resulted from a high room temperature, it might have been possible to prevent its occurrence by adjusting the thermostat or opening the windows. But perhaps the collapse resulted from an improperly digested dinner, or a long-standing physical disability. If so, any attempt to suggest ways in which closure might have been maintained stretches the imagination.

It should also be emphasized that the previous example represents an extreme case. Although all of us could probably agree that the physical collapse of an audience member will influence others' responses to a communication, and although we could readily observe the occurrence of this event, more subtle factors may disturb our closed system of communication. For instance, you may be forced to open the windows to provide a more comfortable room temperature for your audience. Suddenly, the drone of an airplane passing overhead intrudes upon your audience's senses. It so happens that at the previous P.T.A. meeting, a representative from the Office of Civil Defense had explained school-shelter protection in the event of nuclear attack. The sound of the plane serves as a stimulus to generate associations with the previous meeting, and a number of audience members cease to attend to your communication. In this case, the overt stimulus resulting in crucial changes in the internal states of your listeners is not so apparent as a fainting audience member; you may not even be aware that the system has been disturbed by the intrusion of another relevant variable. As a result, you may leave the meeting with an inflated notion of what you have accomplished with the audience.

The value of experimentation. The previous discussion implies that closure is virtually unattainable in a natural, or field, situation. Because of this difficulty, many students of speech communication prefer to study potentially relevant variables within the confines of the laboratory, constructing controlled experiments that enable them to eliminate, or to control, contaminating features of the system. Such undertakings have sometimes led to charges of artificiality; however, those who offer such criticisms are misled concerning the purposes of experimentation. Adherents of laboratory investigation willingly acknowledge that they have eliminated many of the variables present in more "natural" situations. They argue, however, that an understanding of the variables influencing speech communication necessitates a kind of building-block process; i.e., they assert that one must isolate several potentially relevant variables and observe their interaction within a controlled setting. If this is done, it becomes possible to stipulate with some confidence the variables contributing to any observed relationship. On the other hand, a natural setting results in the intrusion of so many variables that it is difficult to identify those which exercise crucial effects. Thus, laboratory researchers subscribe to Homans' statement that "The laws of human behavior are not repealed when a man leaves the field and enters the laboratory";[8] in fact, they hold that the only way in which these laws can be unambiguously determined is in a controlled setting.

The requirement of a closed system therefore dictates a need for controlled laboratory experimentation in speech communication. Even so, everyday communication behavior must continue to take place in natural settings. As a consequence, the impossibility of obtaining closure in such an environment requires that the communicator who

[8] George Caspar Homans, **Social Behavior: Its Elementary Forms** (New York: Harcourt, Brace & World, 1961), p. 15.

is interested in practical decisions about communication strategy scrutinize carefully the characteristics of the situation in which he finds himself. He must be aware that new relevant variables may intrude upon the system at any time, and he must do his best to identify and to adjust to them. He must attend to feedback (a concept discussed more extensively in Chapter 4) and adjust his communication efforts accordingly. Most of all, as has been repeatedly stressed, he must not fall into the trap of oversimplification, of minimizing the psychological complexity of the process in which he is engaged.

The discovery of laws. The requirement of laws has several implications for the student of speech communication. We have defined laws as statements that describe the way in which a specified object will behave in a specified environment. Our previous discussion of closure has demonstrated the difficulties involved in specifying the environment within which a particular communicative act will take place. If we now conceive of sources and receivers as the objects whose behaviors are of interest to us, it becomes equally challenging to specify precisely the relevant factors that will guide their responses. For instance, the hypothetical example of your P.T.A. speech involves a group of objects; i.e., a number of audience members. It would be convenient if a law could be found that would predict the same response for each audience member; e.g., if the source has characteristics **b, c,** and **d,** and if the message contains items **e, f,** and **g,** then the audience member will respond **x.** Whereas this can be done with such physical phenomena as water (e.g., if the water is heated to 212 degrees Fahrenheit and the pressure is standard, then the water will boil), it is not as yet possible to make such predictions about human beings; instead, a speech communication scientist must presently be satisfied with statistical statements about the way **groups** of human beings will behave. Thus, although the general law that deals with the state of water at a temperature of 212 degrees Fahrenheit enables one to deduce that any particular sample of water will behave by boiling, knowledge of the way in which an audience of individuals will respond to a communication does not enable one to make predictions concerning the behavior of an individual member of that audience.

Why does this limitation exist? No relevant individual differences exist that would result in varied reactions when numerous samples of water are placed in an environment in which the temperature is 212 degrees Fahrenheit and the pressure is standard. In other words, the label "water" constitutes a sufficient specification of the object involved in the law. The term "people," however, is an inadequate description of the objects involved in laws pertaining to speech communication. A host of individual differences may cause people to behave differently in the same objective, specified environment. Variations in prior learning experiences produce human beings of varied intellectual abilities, diverse personality traits, and differing beliefs and attitudes. These differences frequently affect the ways in which individuals respond to a communication. Consider again your hypothetical P.T.A. speech. Certainly, you would not expect a conservative, childless, property-owning citizen to respond to a speech advocating passage of a school-bond proposal in the same way in which a liberal renter with three school-age children would react. Even though the objective features of the environment are identical for each of these audience members, it is difficult to conceive of a law that would predict the same behavior for both of them.

The preceding considerations suggest that laws regarding the behavioral effects of speech communication will, of necessity, be quite complex and will depend upon the specification of numerous relevant variables. In addition, it is doubtful that a small set of general laws, capable of predicting any possible behavioral response, can be discovered. Rather, relevant dimensions of both the objects (sources and receivers of speech communication) and the environment (the particular communication situation) will have to be specified in detail, with the result that most response-based laws will apply only to limited groups of sources and receivers.

This is not to say, however, that the student of speech communication cannot profit from the crude generalizations regarding communication behavior that are currently available to him. For instance, although a set of laws regarding source credibility has yet to be formulated, some scientific information exists that demonstrates the importance of this variable.[9] It has been repeatedly demonstrated that highly credible sources elicit more favorable audience response than do sources whose credibility is low. Furthermore, at least some

[9] For a review of much of this research, see Kenneth Andersen and Theodore Clevenger, Jr., "A Summary of Experimental Research in Ethos," **Speech Monographs**, XXX (June 1963), pp. 59–79.

of the major dimensions of credibility are known: the dimensions of competence, trustworthiness, dynamism, and, to some extent, sociability. When analyzing an audience, a speaker can certainly make use of this knowledge, even though he may not know the exact, relative importance of each of the four dimensions of credibility, and even though he may be unable to predict the precise effect of these dimensions on each individual audience member. To say that everything is not known in no way implies that nothing is known, and the student of speech communication should take advantage of available insights, while attempting at the same time to expand further the frontiers of knowledge.

The importance of relevance. The third condition essential for process knowledge—complete sets of relevant variables—carries an implication of major significance to students of speech communication. Here the term "relevant" is of paramount importance, because it indicates that not all variables that occur in the process are crucial to the prediction of communication outcomes. If this were not the case, one could not hope for the development of a science of speech communication.

To illustrate the relative unimportance of some factors, consider two source-associated variables: Social Status and Number of Hairs on Head. Suppose we wish to make predictions concerning a particular source's success with an audience. Do we assume that each of these variables is equally relevant to our prediction? Obviously, we do not. There is good reason to assume that a source's social status influences audience response to his communication, but there is no common-sense reason to believe that the number of hairs on his head should be of any great significance in predicting his communication outcomes.

As with most generalizations, some limitations should be attached to the preceding statement. First, extreme values of the variable, Number of Hairs on Head, may, in fact, influence communication effectiveness. An extremely bushy shock of hair may distract audience members, and a totally bald head may have a similar effect. But these cases are likely to be the exception, rather than the rule; and when they do occur it is possible to adjust our predictions accordingly. On the other hand, the variable of social status will probably be relevant for almost all sources. As a result, a speech communication scientist would be more likely to study the effects of a source's social status on audience response than to vary the number of hairs on a source's head, in order to examine the way in which audience behavior would be influenced by such a manipulation.

Also, the basis for labeling one variable relevant and the other irrelevant must usually be common sense; hence, it is always impossible to say with certainty that a variable is irrelevant. Number of Hairs on Head just **might** influence audience effectiveness; perhaps there is some kind of genetic relationship between quantity of hair and other factors which influence speaking skill. But in the absence of any theoretical or common-sense rationale for suggesting such a relationship, the speech communication scientist assumes that there is not.

Even if these reservations and limitations are taken as given, a significant point emerges: because all variables are probably not relevant to the prediction of communication outcomes, it is not necessary to understand and to isolate all of the variables in the process of speech communication in order to acquire knowledge concerning it. Rather, it is possible to abstract the crucial variables from the process and to study the effects produced by their interactions. This abstracting procedure will be discussed more extensively in Chapter 4.

Summary

This chapter has examined some of the implications of a process viewpoint for the study of speech communication. A definition of process has been stipulated, and the importance of the interaction of variables in determining outcomes of the speech communication process has been emphasized. The three conditions essential to the acquisition of process knowledge—closure of the system, laws, and complete sets of relevant variables—have been discussed, and some of the ways in which each is of interest to students of speech communication have been considered. It has been suggested that the term "relevant variables" is of crucial importance, because it indicates that an understanding of the process of speech communication is not dependent upon a knowledge of all the variables comprising the process.

FOUR

Models and speech communication

The nature of models

The previous chapter pointed out that the complexity of speech communication requires that potentially relevant variables be isolated, or abstracted, from the total process. In accomplishing this task, models of speech communication can be of invaluable assistance. What functions are served by such models? Of equal importance, what are their limitations as aids in studying and understanding speech communication? These questions will be the chief concern of this chapter.

First, however, some of the characteristics of models will be considered; i.e., we will examine some of the salient features of models that are used to depict various aspects of the process of speech communication. Such a discussion is of particular importance because the most common meanings for the term "model" do not correspond to the use applied to the term in this chapter.

Frequently, one thinks of a model as a miniature replica of some larger object or set of objects: an airplane, a gasoline engine, a frontier fort. No doubt this meaning stems from the experience that most of us have had with such models. Furthermore, one often thinks of models not only as replicas, but as **identical** replicas, of the original. For instance, modern hobby kits contain models of gasoline engines that are part by part identical with the original; such models differ only in size, not in detail.

At least two reasons may be cited why a model of speech communication cannot be viewed as an identical replica of the process itself. First, speech communication is a psychological phenomenon, rather than a physical entity. Whereas it is relatively easy to produce physical representations of the parts of a gasoline engine or of an airplane, it is impossible to provide literal analogues for the many overt behaviors and internal responses present in any communicative situation. As a result, a model of speech communication is always symbolic; i.e., it employs words, numbers, or pictures, rather than physical representations, to depict potentially relevant aspects of the process.

Second, the very nature of process also prevents one from viewing a model of speech communication as an identical replica. As has been repeatedly implied, any model of speech communication must, of necessity, focus on only part of the total process. Because it is impossible to construct a model containing all of the variables at work in the process, the model builder must make a conscious selection of the variables that he will include.

Even when it is asserted that a model of speech communication is symbolic, a wide range of possibilities is embraced. Verbal and mathematical models vary tremendously in their sophistication, with these variations depending largely upon how much is known about the particular phenomenon dealt with in the model. In some areas, models function as fully developed and formalized theories from which a number of specific outcomes may be deduced; in fact, certain authors have chosen to view the terms "model" and "theory" as synonymous.[1] Kaplan, however, points out that such usage may not be entirely justified.[2] His concern stems from the belief that only certain types of theories should be labeled as models, but it may, on the contrary, be suggested that many representations that are called models do not meet the tests of a coherent scientific theory. In a sense, such models are little more than useful visual aids.

[1]See, for example, Herbert A. Simon and Allen Newell, "Models: Their Uses and Limitations" in **Current Perspectives in Social Psychology,** eds. Edwin P. Hollander and Raymond G. Hunt (New York: Oxford University Press, 1963), pp. 79–91.
[2]Abraham Kaplan, **The Conduct of Inquiry: Methodology for Behavioral Science** (San Francisco: Chandler, 1964), p. 263.

Given these two extremes (i.e., a developed, formalized theory as opposed to a visual aid), most models of speech communication probably fall closer to the latter extreme than to the former. Even so, such models serve a useful purpose. **Specifically, let us think of a model of the speech communication process as a kind of classificatory system that enables one to abstract and to categorize potentially relevant parts of the process.**

Several considerations are implied by this statement. First, because numerous category systems are readily available, the schema employed will be determined by the purposes and interests of the model builder. It is useful to think of models as arbitrary constructs, as judgments made by the person who creates the model. By adopting this view, one avoids the pitfall of assuming that there is a **correct** model of speech communication; he discards one common meaning for the term "model," i.e., "something eminently worthy of imitation, an exemplar or ideal." Certainly, no present model of speech communication is worthy of such lofty praise.

Second, however, the arbitrary nature of models does not make each one equally valuable. Returning to our stated conception of a model of speech communication, the phrases "classificatory system" and "potentially relevant parts" imply that criteria exist for evaluating a model. The most general criterion is the model's utility. Obviously, some classificatory systems result in more useful categories than others; they allow for greater success in identifying relevant aspects of the process. This point will be considered more fully later in the chapter, when we examine several models that are relevant to students of speech communication.

The functions of models

At their present level of development, most models of the speech communication process serve three major functions: an organizational, or communicative, function; a heuristic, or research-generating, function; and an anticipatory, or predictive, function. Each of these functions is of importance to the student of speech communication, and we will consider them in greater detail.

The organizational function. As stressed in the preceding chapter, a process-oriented individual asserts that speech communication is dynamic, ongoing, and ever-changing. Once he has made this asser tion, however, he has little else to say. As a result of this impasse, it is necessary to provide some organizational framework for talking about the process. A model provides this framework. It enables one to isolate certain relevant dimensions of the process (e.g., a source, a message, and an audience) and to communicate with others about them. Furthermore, such an analysis may be carried further by identifying some of the relevant variables associated with sources, messages, and audiences (e.g., a source's attitudes, his knowledge, his speaking skill). Even though such an undertaking does not capture the entire richness of the process, it is essential to effective communication among students. A model provides the vehicle for this communication.

The heuristic function. A model also serves a heuristic, or research-generating, function. As pointed out earlier, students of speech communication constantly seek to expand the existing frontiers of knowledge, to gain new insights into the complex, psychological process that they are studying. But where does one begin this quest for knowledge? Which variables are to be investigated, and which are to be, at least temporarily, ignored? In order for research to be optimally fruitful, the student must come to grips with the preceding questions; and, in so doing, a model can be of invaluable assistance. Kaplan asserts:

> As inquiry proceeds, theories must be brought out into the open sooner or later; the model simply makes it sooner. In the Socratic metaphor, all thought is the conversation of the soul with itself. The creative imagination, in both scientist and artist, takes the form of a vigorous discussion with the boys in the back room; and there inevitably comes a time when someone says, "Put up or shut up!" It is at this moment that models are brought forward.[3]

Though most models of speech communication are not full-blown, coherent theories, they do represent an intellectual attempt to "Put up or shut up!" That is, they reflect the model builder's thoughts regarding the relevant variables of the process. These variables will receive priority in study and research.

The research-generating function of a model can be illustrated. Figure 2 contains an abbreviated, simple model of the speech communication process. The three major elements of the model are a

---

[3]Ibid., p. 269.

Speaker, a Listener, and Feedback.[4] The model includes two potentially relevant Speaker variables: Attitudes and Encoding[5] Skills; two
Listener variables: Attitudes and Decoding[6] Skills; and two values of
the Feedback variable: Positive and Negative. Let us consider a few
of the many research questions, or hypotheses, suggested by this
simple model.

Figure 2. A simple model of the speech communication process.

For instance, a researcher might hypothesize that the speaker's
encoding skills will influence the listener's attitudes toward the
speaker and toward the proposition that the speaker advocates. Specifically, the researcher might choose to study the encoding variable
Number of Mispronunciations. If he approaches the problem experi-
mentally, this dimension of Encoding Skills becomes the **independent** variable (i.e., the variable that the researcher systematically
manipulates), while the Listener variables of Attitude toward Speaker
(perceived source credibility) and Attitude toward Proposition become the **dependent** variables (i.e., the variables that the researcher
measures). The hypothesis of interest might then be stated as fol-

[4]**Feedback**—those overt responses of a listener that serve to shape and to modify
the succeeding communication behavior of a speaker. Consistent with the
discussion of reward and punishment in Chapter 1, those responses that are
likely to be perceived as rewarding (applause, nods of agreement, apparent
close attention to the message, and so forth) are labeled **positive feedback,**
whereas those responses likely to be perceived as punishing (boos and catcalls,
inattention, yawns, frowns, and so forth) are labeled **negative feedback.**
[5]**Encode**—those psychological activities by which a speaker, or any source of
a communication, translates his internal responses (thoughts, ideas, cognitions)
into observable verbal, vocal, and physical stimuli (messages).
[6]**Decode**—those psychological activities by which a listener, or any receiver of
a communication, translates the observable verbal, vocal, and physical stimuli
of a speaker into internal responses. Usually, although not always, these internal responses result in some subsequent overt behavior.

lows: As the number of mispronunciations presented by a speaker increases, listener attitudes toward the speaker and toward the proposition he advocates will become less favorable. To the extent that this hypothesis is confirmed, the researcher will have discovered a crude law pertaining to the speech communication process.

Numerous other research hypotheses can be generated from the model. Without going into great detail, let us suggest some of them: As listener attitudes toward the speaker become less favorable, a greater quantity of negative feedback will occur. The kind of feedback that a speaker receives will subsequently affect his attitudes and his encoding behaviors. If feedback is predominantly negative, the speaker will manifest a less favorable attitude toward the proposition he advocates; whereas if it is predominantly positive, the converse will occur. Positive feedback will facilitate encoding behavior, and negative feedback will have a disruptive effect on this variable.[7] The more similar the initial attitudes of the speaker and the listener toward the proposition advocated, the greater the amount of positive feedback. These and many other research hypotheses indicate potentially fruitful avenues for investigation.

At this point, it should be emphasized that a model is not a necessary condition for arriving at the preceding hypotheses; each of them could be derived without recourse to the model found in Figure 2. But it is readily apparent that the model provides a classificatory system for organizing and integrating variables, and for making explicit that which was formerly implicit. Also, by omission, the model helps to identify those variables that should **not** be studied. To use a facetious example, it indicates to the researcher that, for the time being, the variable Number of Leprechauns Dancing on the Speaker's Head should be ignored. Given certain conditions, however, this negative function may become a disadvantage of a model, rather than an advantage. These conditions will be discussed in the section below dealing with some potential shortcomings of models.

All interested students of speech communication are not practic-

---

[7]Several studies have demonstrated the existence of this disruptive effect. See John W. Vlandis, "Variations in the Verbal Behavior of a Speaker as a Function of Varied Reinforcing Conditions," **Speech Monographs,** XXXI (June 1964), 116–120; Gerald R. Miller, **et al.,** "The Effect of Differential Reward on Speech Patterns," **Speech Monographs,** XXVIII (March 1961), 9–16; and Gerald R. Miller, "Variations in the Verbal Behavior of a Second Speaker as a Function of Varying Audience Responses," **Speech Monographs,** XXXI (June 1964), 109–116.

ing researchers; instead, many find that questions involving practical communication strategies are of primary interest. What is the best way to encode **this** speech for **this** audience? How can I enhance my credibility with **this** listener, thus increasing the probability of effective communication? How should I respond to **this** particular instance of audience feedback? Each time these questions arise, the communicator will not have the time nor the opportunity to conduct a controlled experiment; rather, he will be forced to make predictions on the basis of the best evidence available.

The anticipatory function. It is in the realm of practical strategy that the third function of models of speech communication, the anticipatory, or predictive function, is of primary significance. Let us return to the hypothetical example of your speech to the P.T.A. group, introduced in Chapter 3. You have just hung up the phone after telling the P.T.A. president that you would speak in favor oî the bond proposal the next evening. Because you are a conscientious communicator and are deeply committed to passage of the proposal, you wish to do everything in your power to ensure that your speech will have maximum audience effect. How can you best accomplish this objective?

Obviously, you will begin to make predictions about the probable characteristics of the environment in which your communication will take place. You will analyze the situation, attempting to identify as many factors as possible that will influence your success. Once again, the classificatory system reflected in a model can assist you greatly. The model serves as a sort of anticipation system, i.e., it helps you to make educated guesses about those factors upon which your success or failure will hinge. Using the simple model in Figure 2 as a reference point, you conclude that you must analyze carefully your listeners' probable initial attitudes toward you and toward the school bond proposal. If their probable attitudes are negative, you must make predictions about the kinds of encoding strategies that are likely to result in favorable changes. You must make judgments about the probable decoding skills of audience members, and you must seek to construct a message in harmony with these abilities. You must remind yourself of the importance of feedback; furthermore, you must make predictions about the kinds of feedback that you are likely to receive, and you must consider ways of adjusting your communication behavior to accommodate the predicted responses. In short, you employ the model as a tool to analyze the situation and to arrive at predictions concerning it.

You could have undertaken this task without depending upon a model of speech communication, but you would probably have been less successful. In a sense, a model serves the same purpose as the conclusion of a syllogism; it explicitly sets forth previously implicit factors and relationships. The importance of this purpose should not be underestimated. The human mind does not function with the speed of an electronic computer; it often fails to grasp implications that are not carefully spelled out. To the extent that a model provides a useful, explicit set of categories for arriving at predictions of communication outcomes, it is indispensable to both the speech communication researcher and to the student of practical communication strategies.

A note of caution. Although we have discussed three functions of models of speech communication, a final note of caution is in order. These functions do not exist as discrete categories; they are closely related. Organization and communication are essential to the effective conduct of research and to the development of predictions concerning probable communication outcomes. The researcher's hypothesis is a prediction, or an anticipation statement, in much the same sense that your educated guesses concerning the probable responses of a particular group of P.T.A. members are predictions. Communication, organization, investigation, prediction, and understanding: all are intimately joined together and all are enhanced by the use of a model of the speech communication process.

Specific models of value

This section will discuss several models of speech communication, in order to present a sample of the purposes for which they are constructed and to demonstrate their importance. The major point to be stressed is that the purposes of the model builder will dictate the elements that appear in the model. To borrow a phrase from dramatic theory, "form follows function"; one must first define the problems with which he wishes to deal. After these problems are identified, it becomes much easier to construct an appropriate model. The models discussed below were formulated to deal with several different types of problems, all of which are relevant to students of speech communication.

Berlo's SMCR model: a general model of the communication process. Certain models have as their major purpose the identification and categorization of variables relevant to the over-all process of communication, i.e., they are general models of the communication process. Berlo's SMCR model, found in Figure 3, is one such model. Let us examine some of its elements in greater detail.

As indicated by Figure 3, the initials S-M-C-R stand for the four major elements in the model: Source, Message, Channel, and Receiver. Source and Receiver variables thought to be especially relevant to the communication process are Communication Skills, Attitudes, Knowledge, the Social System, and the Culture, whereas the factors of Content, Elements, Structure, Code, and Treatment are viewed as essential Message variables. In this model, Channels are conceived of as sense modalities rather than communication media; consequently, the Channels listed are the senses of Seeing, Hearing, Touching, Smelling, and Tasting. Although several statements in Berlo's volume attest to the importance of feedback, this concept is not incorporated into the model itself.

An examination of the model reveals that it is potentially applicable to any communicative act, whether written or spoken. It could be used as a tool for analyzing the situation involved in your hypothetical speech to P.T.A. audience members, and it could also be of assistance in arriving at predictions about the most effective strategies to utilize when writing a letter of application to a prospective employer. In this respect, the terms "Source" and "Receiver" are more general than the labels "Speaker" and "Listener," employed in the abbreviated model found in Figure 2, because they apply to encoders and decoders of both written and spoken messages.

The SMCR model serves each of the three functions of speech communication models already discussed. By abstracting certain relevant parts, Berlo's model provides a means for communicating about dimensions of the total process. For example, one can now discuss a communication source and consider some of the potential factors that may influence his effectiveness. Likewise, constituent elements of the message can be identified and communicated to others. To be sure, one can always question whether all of the relevant variables have been incorporated into the model, or even

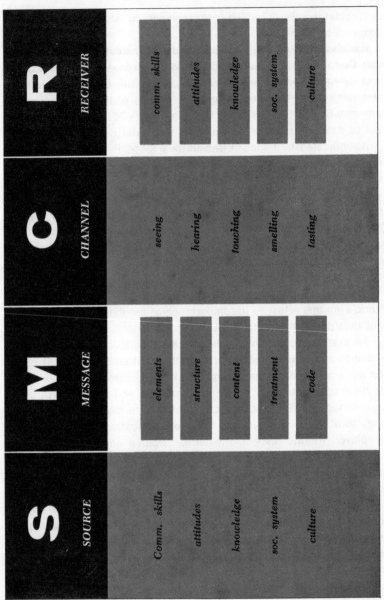

Figure 3. The SMCR Model.

whether the ones selected are those of greatest importance; however, the primary point is that the model enables one to go from broad generalizations to more specific statements about various aspects of the process.

That the model serves a research-generating function can be readily demonstrated. Numerous research questions or hypotheses are suggested by the variables found in the model, particularly because almost any of them could be studied as either independent or dependent variables. Thus, one could systematically vary the number of channels employed in the communication (independent variable) and measure the effects on the receiver's knowledge level or attitudes (dependent variable). It would be possible to manipulate the treatment of message content (independent variable), in order to study the way in which the receiver's attitudes are influenced (dependent variable); or different initial attitudes could be induced in sources (independent variable), and the messages that they encode could be analyzed for potential differences in treatment (dependent variable). Actually, the number of possible research alternatives is extremely large. In addition, the investigator is not limited to a single independent variable; he may select several of the source variables stipulated in the model and manipulate these variables in combination to determine their joint effect on some dependent measure. This latter procedure enables him to arrive at more complex generalizations than are possible through manipulation of a single variable; it opens the door to discovery of higher-order laws.

Finally, the predictive function served by the model can assist both the speech communication researcher and the practitioner. Analysis of the major elements and of the variables encompassed under each of these elements will assist the student in predicting probable communication outcomes and in arriving at strategies likely to result in maximum behavioral effect. As a result, the model can be used as a guideline for planning and executing particular communicative acts.

What questions or criticisms regarding the SMCR model can be advanced? The model has been criticized because of its failure to reflect the process nature of communication. As the earlier discussion of the nature of models would imply, this indictment is rather naive. By definition, no model of spoken or written communication can provide an accurate image of the complete process; instead, the

model must be viewed as an abstraction of selected, potentially relevant dimensions of the whole. To demand the quality of complete-
ness for a model demonstrates a fundamental misunderstanding of
its nature and functions.

One can, of course, argue more validly that the SMCR model is
not the most useful and accurate abstraction that could have been
constructed, that certain variables should have been omitted and
certain others included. For instance, the author believes that any
model that is process-oriented should include the concept of feedback; its omission from the SMCR schema represents at least a
minor shortcoming. As already pointed out, however, Berlo generally
stresses the importance of feedback, and another of his models, the
Interpreter, makes reference to this concept.[8]

Over-all, an individual's reaction to the SMCR model, or to any
general model of communication, will reflect his own interests and
purposes. Other general communication models, both more and less
complex than the SMCR model, are available. Once one's objectives
have been determined, a careful analysis of several of these models
should reveal which has the greatest utility, and this consideration
should dictate the best selection.

**Kelman's three processes of social influence: a model dealing
with a particular communication problem.** Whereas the SMCR model
is intended as a general model of communication, a number of other
models attempt to deal with specific, limited communication problems. One such attempt is represented by Kelman's model of the
three processes of social influence. The model itself can best be
introduced by an initial consideration of the problem with which it
deals, a problem of considerable significance to students of speech
communication.

For illustration, let us again turn to your hypothetical speech to
the P.T.A. audience. Assume that you have presented the speech and
that you are now striving to ascertain the extent of its effect. To
accomplish this end, you ask several of the audience members how
they feel about the bond proposal. Each of them responds, "Your
speech totally convinced us. We will give one hundred per cent support to the proposal." You find this reaction both satisfying and
flattering, but you are still plagued by a nagging doubt that some of

[8]David K. Berlo, **The Process of Communication** (New York: Holt, Rinehart and
Winston, 1960), pp. 99–106.

your receivers do not really believe what they have told you. You reason that their commitment may be entirely due to your presence, and you fear that once you have departed the scene they may abandon their promised support.

The essence of the problem posed in the preceding paragraph, a problem of major interest to students of speech communication, can be phrased: **Under what conditions does the response of an individual to a communication reflect only a public behavior, and under what conditions does it reflect an accompanying private belief?** In other words, how is it possible to ascertain whether or not a person really believes what he says?

Before proceeding further, the ambiguity of the phrase "really believes" invites clarification. When one asserts that another does not really believe something, it sounds almost as though the person making the assertion has direct access to the other's mental contents, that he can "read the other's mind." Obviously, this is not the most defensible meaning that can be assigned to the phrase. Instead, what is usually meant is that at a certain time and place the individual made a particular statement (e.g., that he favored the bond proposal), and at some later time he uttered a different assertion (e.g., that he opposed the proposal or that he was indifferent toward it). The assumption has then been made that one of the two behaviors is a more accurate reflection of the individual's private beliefs. Actually, because the only evidence available to us is the individual's conflicting behavior, the assumption contains the only referential meaning that the statement can have—it would be rather absurd to talk of one behavior as more "real" than another.

Often, the crucial factor leading to varying responses at different times is the presence or absence of some other person in the environment. Thus, in our example, it was suggested that your presence in the environment might result in choruses of support for the bond proposal, whereas in your absence the same individuals might trigger opposition or plead indifference. In fact, such a situation represents the way chosen by Kelman to distinguish between public conformity and private acceptance. He asserts:

> Measurement under public conditions does not simply mean that the subject's [subject can be considered synonymous with receiver or audience member] responses will be observed by **someone,** but rather that they will be observed by some **specific** individual or group—gen-

erally the influencing agent [Kelman's term for source], or the group whose normative expectations the subject would wish to meet. **Measurement under private conditions in a literal sense is, of course, impossible, since the measurement situation requires the subject to express himself publicly** [boldface mine]. What is meant here is that the subject's attitudes are ascertained in a situation in which he presumably has no reason for distorting his private beliefs. Usually this is accomplished by creating a situation in which the subject can feel that his responses are **in effect** private. This would be true if the subject is assured of anonymity, or if the subject has no reason to believe that his responses will be observed by those individuals or groups whose expectations he might wish to meet. **Whether these are "really" his private beliefs is an unanswerable question. For our purposes, public vs. private conditions refers to conditions in which the subject's behavior is vs. those in which it is not observable by the effective influencing agent** [boldface mine].[9]

Thus, in terms of the hypothetical P.T.A. speech, the attitudes of your listeners toward the bond proposal might be sampled in one or more of several ways. Following the speech, you could ask all of the audience members who favor the proposal to raise their hands, or you could ask each of them to write "For" or "Against" on a slip of paper, sign his name on the slip, and hand it to you. Conditions such as these are obviously public, i.e., each audience member knows that his behavior is being observed by you, the influence agent. You could, however, ask each of them to write "For" or "Against" on a slip of paper and to hand it in without signing his or her name. This condition is more private than the first two; assuming that they have no reason to believe that you can recognize their handwriting or that you have coded the slips so that they can be associated with particular individuals, the listeners feel they will remain anonymous. Finally, you could leave, and another individual could ask the audience members to express their attitudes anonymously, stressing the fact that you will neither see nor subsequently know their responses. This condition insures maximum privacy, for your physical absence and the anonymity of the response makes it seem highly probable to your audience that you will not know their behaviors.

Under the conditions described, several alternative courses of

[9]Herbert C. Kelman, "Social Influence and Personal Belief: A Theoretical and Experimental Approach to the Study of Behavioral Change." From an unpublished manuscript, "Social Influence and Personal Belief," 2.16–2.17.

action are available to audience members. They may express unfavorable attitudes toward the bond proposal both under public and private conditions of response. If this occurred, your attempt to exert behavioral influence would have been totally unsuccessful. On the other hand, they may agree with you in your presence (public conditions) but disagree in your absence or under conditions of anonymity (private conditions). If this occurred, you would probably feel that you had been only partially successful in your attempt to alter their responses. It is also possible that these listeners may express favorable attitudes under public and private conditions of response, but that the effect in the latter situation will be relatively short-lived. Thus, following your speech, they may respond favorably in your absence (private conditions), only to vote "No" on the proposal two weeks later. Again, your influence attempt has been less than optimally successful. Finally, audience members may react favorably both publicly and privately, with the latter effects proving to be relatively stable and enduring; i.e., they may vote "Yes" on the forthcoming proposal. In this case, you would have satisfactorily accomplished your objective in communicating with this group; your speech communication would have achieved the desired behavioral effect.

Kelman is primarily interested in predicting which of the above results will occur for any particular influence attempt; in other words, he seeks to identify the variables that will enable him to predict the conditions under which a communication-induced response will be adopted, the conditions under which it will be retained, and the conditions under which it will be abandoned. His model represents an attempt to specify these variables; and, as such, it is a model constructed to deal with a special problem of significance to students of speech communication.

Kelman posits three distinct processes of social influence: Compliance, Identification, and Internalization. Each process has several antecedent and consequent conditions associated with it. The antecedent and consequent conditions for each of the three processes are summarized in the model found in the table on page 66. Rather than deal with each of these conditions, let us examine each of the three processes with reference to the importance of one antecedent condition, "Source of power of the influencing agent," and one consequent condition, "Conditions of performance of induced response." This limited treatment should illustrate the relevance of the model to the study of speech communication, but the reader who wishes a more extensive discussion should consult Kelman's writings.

SUMMARY OF DISTINCTIONS AMONG THE THREE PROCESSES

Antecedents:	*Compliance*	*Identification*	*Internalization*
1. Basis for the **importance of the induction**	Concern with social effect of behavior	Concern with social anchorage of behavior	Concern with value congruence of behavior
2. Source of **power of the influencing agent**	Means-control	Attractiveness	Credibility
3. Manner of achieving **prepotency of the induced response**	Limitation of choice behavior	Delineation of role requirements	Reorganization of means-ends framework
Consequents:			
1. Conditions of performance of induced response	Surveillance by influencing agent	Salience of relationship to agent	Relevance of values to issue
2. Conditions of change and extinction of induced response	Changed perception of conditions for social rewards	Changed perception of conditions for satisfying self-defining relationships	Changed perception of conditions for value maximization
3. Type of behavior system in which induced response is embedded	External demands of a specific setting	Expectations defining a specific role	Person's value system

Reproduced by permission from Kelman, Herbert C., "Processes of Opinion Change," **Public Opinion Quarterly,** XXV (Spring 1961), 67.

For Kelman, Compliance occurs when "an individual adopts behavior derived from another person or group because he hopes to achieve a favorable reaction from the other."[10] In an influence situ-

[10]Herbert C. Kelman, "Compliance, Identification, and Internalization: A Theoretical and Experimental Approach to the Study of Social Influence." Preliminary draft of a monograph in preparation, National Institute of Mental Health, 1956, p. 17.

ation dominated by Compliance, the individual performs the induced behavior "not because he believes in the content of the behavior, but because he expects to gain specific rewards or approval and avoid punishments or disapproval by conforming."[11]

Let us translate your communication to the P.T.A. into a compliant situation for certain audience members. Assume that you own a local business and that these particular audience members are your employees. Further, grant that you are known to be a rigid, intolerant individual who becomes quite irritated when others disagree with your ideas, a person who is not adverse to rewarding those who conform to your expectations and to punishing those who do not. You have just presented a speech advocating passage of a school-bond proposal, and you have requested that those who agree with you raise their hands or indicate agreement in writing on slips of paper bearing their names. It is easy to see how those audience members in your employ would perceive this as a compliant situation.

In this example, the importance of the antecedent, "Source of power of the influencing agent," is readily apparent. "To the extent to which the power of the influencing agent is based on means-control, conformity will tend to take the form of compliance."[12] Further, "an influencing agent may be perceived as possessing means-control because of his **actual** control over specific rewards and punishments."[13] Thus, to the extent that you can reward employees by giving them more desirable positions in the company, by granting them substantial raises, or by keeping their work loads light, your source of power as an influence agent is based on means-control. It is likely that those audience members who work for you will publicly subscribe to, or comply with, your beliefs; on the other hand, in this particular context, you will not be able to exercise means-control over the remaining members of the group. Of course, it is possible that various other factors will enable you to motivate compliant behavior on the part of other listeners; e.g., some additional audience members may be local businessmen who hope to obtain a highly profitable contract from you.

It should be obvious that compliant behavior occurs only under public conditions of response. This fact is emphasized by the sur-

[11]**Ibid.**
[12]**Ibid.**, p. 95.
[13]**Ibid.**

veillance variable associated with the consequent "Conditions of performance of induced response." Kelman asserts that "when an individual adopts an induced response through compliance, he tends to perform it only under conditions of surveillance by the influencing agent"; that is, "if the influencing agent is physically present, or if it is known to the individual that—in some way or another—the agent will find out what the behavior has been."[14] In your hypothetical role of tyrannical employer, your influence is dependent upon your knowledge of the behaviors of those audience members for whom you exercise means-control. Although they may express acceptance of your ideas when you are physically present, it is probable that in the privacy of the voting booth they will vote "No" on the proposal.

How does the second process, Identification, differ from Compliance? "Identification can be said to occur when an individual adopts behavior derived from another person or a group because this behavior is associated with a satisfying self-defining relationship to this person or group."[15] Performing the induced response to identify "is a way of establishing or maintaining the desired relationship to the other, and the self-definition which is anchored in this relationship."[16]

In other words, individuals sometimes perform induced behaviors because of their desire to "be like" the influence agent, because they perceive in him desirable qualities to which they aspire. The agent becomes a sort of model for behavior, primarily because of his attractive traits. Thus, in your audience of P.T.A. members, some listeners may view you as a prestigeful, attractive communicator, even though you do not possess any means-control over them. The rewards that these audience members gain from conforming to your expressed attitudes do not result from your direct control over their outcomes, but rather from the intrinsic satisfaction to be gained from establishing a favorable relationship with you.

As already indicated, influence based on Identification is dependent upon the antecedent of an attractive influence agent. It must be possible for the agent "to provide a satisfying relationship for the individual."[17] If the P.T.A. members feel that they would derive little satisfaction from a relationship with you, it is doubtful that the need for Identification would be compelling enough to produce the desired

[14]Ibid., p. 106.
[15]Ibid., p. 28.
[16]Ibid.
[17]Ibid., p. 96.

behavior. "Conformity will tend to take the form of identification" only "to the extent to which the power of the influencing agent is based on attractiveness."[18]

Although behavior adopted because of Identification is not completely at the public level, it does not qualify as a stable, privately held belief. The key to this rather enigmatic statement is found in the necessary consequent of salience. "When an individual adopts an induced response through identification, he tends to perform it only under conditions of salience[19] of his relationship to the agent."[20] Salience exists if this relationship is so defined "that the individual acts within the particular role which is involved in identification and with which the induced response is associated."[21] Thus, stated loosely, it may not be necessary for the agent to be **physically** present, but it is definitely required that he be **psychologically** present; i.e., that there exists a link between the induced behavior and the role relationship with which it is associated. Such a situation is represented by the case in which an audience member expresses immediate support for the bond proposal under both public and private conditions of response, but votes "No" two weeks later. At that time, the relationship with which the response is associated is no longer salient; hence, he reverts back to his original belief.

Only the third process, Internalization, results in a stable private belief. As a result, it is the kind of influence that all of us, in our roles as oral communicators, hope to exert. "Internalization can be said to occur when an individual adopts behavior derived from another person or a group because he finds the content of that behavior satisfying."[22] An individual who internalizes "adopts induced behavior because he believes it to be valid or correct."[23] Thus, Internalization not only produces the most durable effects, it conforms most closely to a rational, ethically desirable concept of persuasion. Ideally, it is hoped that the P.T.A. members will vote for the proposal because it makes good sense and because they respect your good

[18]**Ibid.**, p. 95.
[19]**Salience**—psychological prominence, i.e., a stimulus in the environment is said to be salient if there are a number of cues to remind the individual of that stimulus or if the stimulus itself is a prominent and distinctive element of the environment.
[20]**Ibid.**, p. 106.
[21]**Ibid.**, p. 108.
[22]**Ibid.**, p. 19.
[23]**Ibid.**

judgment, not because they are fearful of you or because you have overwhelmed them with your magnetic personality.

In order for Internalization to occur, the influence agent must be perceived as highly credible. An influence agent possesses credibility "if his statements are considered truthful and valid, and hence worthy of serious consideration."[24] As a result, P.T.A. audience members who perceived you as qualified and expert because of your previous community activities, your prior service on committees dealing with educational problems, or your previous professional training in educational administration would indicate support of the bond issue primarily because of the validity of your opinions and the "good sense" of the proposal itself.

As pointed out, the consequent condition required for performance of an internalized response differs markedly from those required for Compliance and Identification. Kelman asserts that "when an individual adopts an induced response through internalization, he tends to perform it under conditions of relevance to the issue, and regardless of surveillance or salience."[25] Thus, once the response has been adopted, its subsequent performance becomes independent of the influencing agent, i.e., it is performed in the agent's physical and psychological absence. Such a situation insures not only that favorable attitudes toward the bond proposal will be immediately expressed under both public and private conditions, but that those professing such attitudes will also vote "Yes" at the election two weeks later. In fact, these favorable attitudes should be demonstrated at any time in the future when the issue is of relevance.

Though all of the implications of Kelman's model have not been discussed, some of its more salient features should be emphasized. First, it can be seen that the model deals specifically with the problem of public versus privately held beliefs; and, as stated earlier, it attempts to specify the conditions under which a communication-induced response will be adopted, the conditions under which it will be retained, and the conditions under which it will be abandoned. Thus, if a potential influence agent does not possess any of the three sources of power, he will be unsuccessful in motivating the audience to adopt the recommended behaviors. If his power stems from means-control or from attractiveness, the behaviors will be performed under public conditions of response (i.e., when the agent is

[24]Ibid., p. 97.
[25]Ibid., p. 106.

physically and/or psychologically present) and abandoned under private conditions. But if the agent's power stems from credibility, the behaviors will be performed under both public and private conditions of response; they will become an enduring part of the individual's belief system.

Like all other models dealing with speech communication, Kelman's three processes represent an abstraction and an oversimplification of the total process. Obviously, many communicators possess all three sources of power: they are in a position to exercise means-control over their receivers; they are perceived as attractive by audience members; and they are viewed by listeners as highly credible sources. As indicated, this could be the case with your hypothetical P.T.A. speech. In most communication situations, a subtle intermingling of the three processes will take place. Even so, careful analysis should enable the student to identify relevant features of each of the three processes in most ongoing communication situations.

That Kelman's model serves the three functions delegated to models of speech communication need not be belabored. Obviously, the model enables one to communicate more effectively about the dynamics of the problem with which it deals. It has already served to generate a body of empirical research, and more is in the offing.[26] Finally, it can be of assistance in arriving at predictions regarding practical communication strategies and in suggesting methods by which one might enhance the probability of a response being internalized by a listener.

Because of their relevance to students of speech communication, Kelman's three processes have been discussed in some detail. The processes deal with a problem of importance to communication, that of distinguishing between publicly and privately held beliefs. Also, and of equal importance, the model illustrates how effectively specific, particular problems may be handled with the aid of a theoretical, procedural framework.

A model of nonverbal communication: an essential aspect of the process of speech communication. Thus far, speech communication has been treated largely as "talk," as a process in which a source employs language to elicit certain meanings on the part of his receivers. Obviously, however, the process of speech communication

---

[26]See, for example, Herbert C. Kelman, "Compliance, Identification, and Internalization: Three Processes of Attitude Change," **Journal of Conflict Resolution**, II (March 1958), 51–60.

contains much that is nonverbal: the facial expressions of the communicator, his movements and gestures, the volume, rate, and tone
of his voice. These and many other factors are a vital part of the
total message decoded by the receiver; and, together, they function
to increase or to decrease the probability that the communicator will
achieve his desired behavioral effect.

Assume that in your hypothetical P.T.A. speech you say: "I know
that each of you is keenly aware of the importance of adequate educational facilities, and that you are intelligent enough to realize that
this bond proposal is essential to the provision of these facilities."
How greatly will your physical behavior and tone of voice affect the
meaning elicited by these particular verbal symbols? The answer to
this question is obvious. Suppose that while uttering the statement,
you allow a scornful sneer to appear on your face. Or that you speak
in a condescending or sarcastic tone of voice. Or that you make the
statement in a jocular manner, with an accompanying wink of the
eye. In each instance, you would expect the audience members to
respond differently, to supply varied meanings for the same set of
verbal stimuli.

Although most students agree that these nonverbal behaviors are
a vital element of the process of speech communication, less research has been carried out concerning their effects than has been
done concerning verbal stimuli. Practical problems are involved in
designing sound investigations and experiments. When compared
with the verbal aspects of a message, subtle nuances in gesture or
facial expression are more difficult to manipulate and to control.
Modern technological developments are, however, helping to allevi-
ate this problem; for example, it is now practical to make video tapes
of speakers in which certain nonverbal aspects of their presentations
can be systematically varied.

The importance of these nonverbal factors of communication is
emphasized by the model found in Figure 4.[27] It can be seen that the

[27] I am grateful to my colleague, Randall P. Harrison, whose model of pictorial
communication provided a basis for the development of this model. Harrison
has written extensively on problems of pictorial and other nonverbal modes of
communication. See, for example, "Pictic Analysis: Toward a Vocabulary and
Syntax for the Pictorial Code; With Research on Facial Communication." Unpublished Ph.D. Dissertation, Michigan State University, 1964; and "Nonverbal
Communication: Explorations into Time, Space, Action, and Object" in **Dimensions in Communication,** eds. James H. Campbell and Hal W. Hepler (Belmont, California: Wadsworth, 1965), pp. 158–174.

Source-Encoder constructs a message concerning some Referent. In order to avoid confusion, it should be pointed out that the term "Referent" is employed in a broader sense than is usual. Specifically, the Source-Encoder constructs a message that may "refer to" a wide range of objects, acts, situations, ideas, or experiences: the Referents. Returning to the hypothetical P.T.A. speech, the entire social, economic, and political milieu surrounding the educational system and the bond proposal can serve as message Referents.

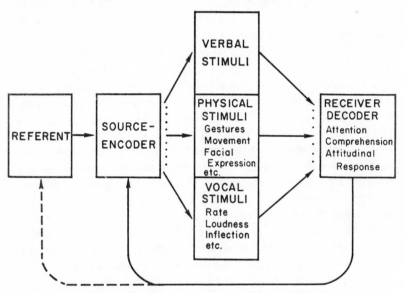

Figure 4. A model emphasizing nonverbal communication.

The total message that is encoded consists of at least three principal factors: Verbal Stimuli, Physical Stimuli, and Vocal Stimuli. Although these are linked with the Source-Encoder by three separate arrows, the joining of these arrows with dotted lines indicates that all three dimensions of the message are encoded simultaneously, and that the message functions as a unit.

The message is transmitted to a Receiver-Decoder, who responds in some way to its verbal, physical, and vocal elements. As indicated, the first motive of the Source-Encoder is to gain the Receiver's attention. Once his attention is focused on the message, the Receiver-Decoder supplies a set of meanings for it, and certain nonevaluative

(Comprehension) and evaluative (Attitudinal) responses occur. The extent to which these responses are consistent with the Source-Encoder's purpose is dependent upon the total meaning resulting from the particular combination of the three types of stimuli. The arrows extending from the Receiver-Decoder to the Source-Encoder and to the Referent indicate that the Receiver-Decoder may respond jointly to at least two categories of stimuli: those linked with the Referent itself (primarily the Verbal Stimuli) and those associated with the individual who is encoding statements about the Referent (primarily the Physical and Vocal Stimuli). Obviously, the Receiver-Decoder's responses to both Source-Encoder and Referent will interact to determine the meaning he assigns to the situation. Whereas it would be psychologically difficult to respond to the Referent without also responding to the Source-Encoder, the converse does not necessarily hold; i.e., the Receiver-Decoder might focus his entire attention on the Physical and Vocal Stimuli encoded by the Source and largely ignore the Verbal Stimuli relating to the Referent.

The most obvious potential problem faced by the Source-Encoder consists of potential disparities in the meanings assigned by the Receiver-Decoder to the three sets of message factors. For instance, in speaking to the P.T.A., you might assert that "This school-bond proposal is the most crucial issue ever faced by our community." If you made this statement in a tired, flat voice, and if your bodily posture appeared to be relaxed or lethargic, it is probable that the intended meaning would not be elicited from your audience. Or if you remarked that "The increase in taxes will not place an excessive burden on any of you," while gazing furtively out of the window, a disastrous audience response would possibly result. In short, effective communication depends upon the harmonious blending of Verbal, Physical, and Vocal Stimuli.

A general problem area for research suggested by the model has to do with the relationships between Verbal and Physical and Vocal Stimuli. Which combinations of these stimuli will elicit the intended meaning (in a sense, which combinations of stimuli are psychologically consistent), and which will result in meanings inconsistent with the purpose of the Source-Encoder? Common sense offers some tentative answers to this question, but these common-sense assumptions should be buttressed by empirical research. The relative importance of each of the three factors is yet to be determined.

Although they undoubtedly function conjunctively, it is not necessarily true that each factor is equally important in determining the meaning elicited. Individual difference variables are also relevant; e.g., certain audience members may place greatest emphasis on Vocal Stimuli, and others may attend primarily to Physical Stimuli. Each of these possibilities provides fertile grounds for investigation by speech communication researchers.

It can be seen that this model of nonverbal communication also satisfies the other two major functions delegated to models of speech communication: it provides a framework for communicating about selected aspects of the process, and it enables one to develop predictions about the probable outcomes of certain communication strategies. Most important, however, the model emphasizes nonverbal factors of speech communication; it again reinforces the assertion that the elements and structure of a model are dependent upon the purposes of the model builder.

This section began with a discussion of the arbitrary nature of speech communication models, and it would be well to close by re-emphasizing this point. It would be fruitless for the student of speech communication to seek the one true, correct model of speech communication, but he should be aware that there are numerous models that can aid him in analyzing and understanding the total process. Let him not limit his vistas by selecting any one of these; but, rather, let him expand his horizons by making use of the appropriate and relevant features of each.

Some potential shortcomings of models

Thus far, we have stressed that models can be of invaluable assistance to the student of speech communication. This endorsement should now be tempered. The most useful tool may be treated shoddily, and any intellectual device can be misused almost as readily as it can be used to advantage. What are some of the potential shortcomings of models of speech communication? Specifically, this section will consider three intimately related shortcomings: premature closure, symbol-behavior confusion, and oversimplification.[28]

Premature closure. You will recall that one of the essential condi-

---

[28]A more extensive list of shortcomings, along with a more extensive discussion of each, can be found in Kaplan, **The Conduct of Inquiry,** pp. 275–288.

tions for the acquisition of process knowledge is closure of the system, i.e., the ability to prevent the intrusion of potentially relevant variables into the system. In a sense, a model imposes intellectual closure on the system, because it stipulates the variables that are to be studied and those that are to be ignored. As previously emphasized, the very nature of a model makes this restriction both necessary and desirable; but, under certain circumstances, closure can be a detriment, rather than an asset. This is particularly true in an area such as speech communication, where so little is yet known about the subject matter.

Consider again the simple model introduced at the beginning of this chapter (Figure 2), a model having as its major elements: Speaker, Listener, and Feedback. You will recall that two Speaker variables, Attitudes and Encoding Skills, and two Listener variables, Attitudes and Decoding Skills, are found in the model. Assume that research based on this model uncovers some simple relationship, e.g., that a listener whose attitudes toward the topic are similar to those of the speaker will learn more message content than a listener whose attitudes toward the topic vary from those of the speaker. Later, however, it is found that this relationship holds only part of the time. Further, assume that the other relevant variable, Decoding Skills, is relatively constant for all listeners; i.e., that they do not differ greatly in intelligence, listening skills, etc. If I am the researcher employing the model, how can I explain the inconsistent results that I have obtained?

At least two alternatives are at my disposal. If I wish to retain my present model **in toto,** I can argue that the results are not inconsistent at all; rather, in those instances in which the relationship did not hold, some experimental source of error contaminated my findings. For instance, my attitude measurement may not have discriminated accurately on all occasions, or my retention test may not have been a consistently valid measure of learning. In other words, if I so choose, I can refuse to change the system being studied in any way, and I can focus my attention on the probable sources of error that confound my findings.

My second alternative is to admit that the model is inadequate to deal with the problem, that another relevant variable, or variables, may be influencing some of the outcomes that I have observed. If I make this admission, I am granting that premature closure has been imposed on the system, i.e., that an attempt has been made to explain a communication phenomenon without taking into account certain relevant variables that affect it. My next step is either to abandon, or, more probably, to revise my present model, in order to include those variables that may be influencing my results. By so doing, I may find that differences in the variable of, say, Socio-Economic Status are the crucial factor, and that when I incorporate this variable into the experiment I can better explain my obtained results.

To many, it may seem that any sensible man would seize the second alternative; however, it should be remembered that psychological factors often lead us to commit ourselves firmly to a specific course of action or to a particular theoretical viewpoint. Commitment to a model may result in the same kind of behavior. As Kaplan has asserted:

> Closure is premature if it lays down the lines for our thinking to follow when we do not know enough to say even whether one direction or another is the more promising. Building a model, in short, may crystallize our thoughts at a stage when they are much better left in solution, to allow new compounds to precipitate.[29]

For this reason, models should be used flexibly; they should not be regarded as one-hundred-per-cent truth, pure in grade. To impose premature closure is to retard, rather than to accelerate, the study of speech communication.

Symbol-behavior confusion. A model is a representation of selected dimensions of the process; it is not the process itself. On the surface, this statement seems self-evident. Even so, confusion of symbol with thing, as the general semanticist constantly reminds us, is quite common among human beings. Thus, a model of speech communication may lull us into the false belief that because we have named a variable we have explained it, or, at an even more elementary level, isolated it. Moreover, in a different vein, we may be led to believe that the more erudite and learned our symbols, notations, and definitions, the more cogent our explanation of the behaviors involved in the process. Kaplan has attacked this latter error effectively, stating:

> Unfortunately, in behavioral science it is not uncommon that the symbolic style is only a mode of expression and not of thought. In a manner of speaking, it is often nothing but a manner of speaking.

[29]Kaplan, p. 279.

> Definitions abound, but they are pseudo definitions: they do not specify
> the ways in which the defined terms are actually used in what follows.
> Elaborate notations often only codify the obvious, and though the
> symbols may be more economical . . . what they achieve is hardly
> worth the trouble.[30]

Although few models of speech communication have been reduced
to mathematical propositions of the type that Kaplan is criticizing,
esoteric jargon is frequently substituted for perfectly good words,
sometimes on the assumption that such substitutions enhance
explanation of the behavioral process itself. This tendency should be
avoided whenever possible.

Let us approach the point in another way. To label a variable
"Attitude" and to define it as "a learned predisposition to respond
positively or negatively" does little to explain the ways in which
attitudinal behaviors influence the process of speech communication.
Such an approach frequently leads to circular reasoning; e.g., one
may say that an individual responded to a speech in a particular
way because of a certain attitude that he held. When pressed for
evidence that the individual held this attitude, the commentator may
invoke as proof the individual's original response to the speech. Or,
at a more absurd level, consider the facetious variable mentioned
earlier, Number of Leprechauns Dancing on the Speaker's Head.
One could build such a variable into a model of speech communication and suggest that there is a relationship between that variable
and speaker effectiveness. Furthermore, in every instance of ineffec-
tive communication, it could be argued that the Leprechaun variable
was the crucial determinant. Such a procedure is clearly in error.
Although a verbal concept has been stipulated, it is certainly not
synonymous with a behavior; and, in this particular instance, it is
impossible to specify clearly any behavior to which it corresponds.

There is no need to stress further the shortcoming of symbol-
behavior confusion. A distinguished sociologist, George Homans, has
written caustically that "much modern sociological theory seems . . .
to possess every virtue except that of explaining anything."[31] If one
is trapped by symbol-behavior confusion, models of speech communication may suffer from the same problem: they may become

[30]Ibid., p. 278.
[31]George Caspar Homans, **Social Behavior: Its Elementary Forms** (New York:
Harcourt, Brace & World, Inc., 1961), p. 10.

elaborate linguistic or pictorial devices that bear no real relationship to the behavioral process with which they purport to deal.

Oversimplification. To simplify the complex process of speech communication is a necessity; to oversimplify it may perpetrate an intellectual and a practical injustice. As suggested in the discussion of premature closure, it may often be preferable to stumble half-blindly through the labyrinth of process, rather than to create a false illusion of simplicity through the construction of a model. Again, much is dependent upon the particular form taken by the oversimplification. If essential elements are included, then simplification is a virtue, rather than a fault, but "it is one thing to ignore certain features of a complex reality on the hypothesis that what is being neglected is not essential, at least to a first approximation. It is quite another thing . . . to simplify in a particular way because then the model would be so much more elegant, or so much easier to work with."[32]

For example, one may feel that the simple model containing the elements of Speaker, Listener, and Feedback is a sufficient first approximation of the process of speech communication. To the extent that this is true, the oversimplification involved is not a detriment. If, however, only these three elements have been included because of an intellectual fear of a more complex model, the chances are excellent that the model's simplicity grossly distorts the workings of the total process. If this is the case, the model builder has equipped himself with intellectual blinders.

As mentioned earlier, the three potential shortcomings that have been discussed are intimately related. Both premature closure and symbol-behavior confusion may result in oversimplification. In utilizing models, the student should avoid each of these pitfalls. Failure to do so will greatly reduce the model's value as a tool for analyzing and understanding the complex behavioral process of speech communication.

Summary

This chapter has considered the functions of models in the study of speech communication. Following some preliminary remarks on the nature of models, three primary functions of speech communica-

[32]Kaplan, p. 280.

tion models were suggested: an organizational, or communicative function; heuristic, or research-generating function, and an anticipatory, or predictive function. Several representative models of relevance to speech communication were discussed, stressing that the elements and structure of a model are dependent upon the purposes of the model builder. Finally, three potential shortcomings of models of speech communication—premature closure, symbol-behavior confusion, and oversimplification—were introduced; and the importance of avoiding these pitfalls was emphasized.

FIVE

Ethics and speech communication

The major ethical problems of speech communication

Except for the discussion of the ethical dimension of purpose found in Chapter 2, I have not as yet departed from my primary purpose of developing a viewpoint concerning the behavioral dimension of speech communication. Consistent with the secondary objective stated at the conclusion of Chapter 1, this final chapter will consider briefly some value judgments that are intimately related to the behavioral matters discussed throughout this volume. The reader will recall earlier brief encounters with some of these judgments; however, by reintroducing them here, I hope to underscore their importance to all students of speech communication.

Two major ethical problems dominate the field of speech communication, both dependent upon the validity of this assumption: **All human behavior is lawfully determined; therefore, knowledge of the laws that determine an individual's response to a communication enables the one possessing this knowledge to exercise behavioral control over others.** If the assumption is correct, the following questions are of vital importance:

1. What, if any, are the ethical responsibilities of the individual who strives to discover new knowledge about the laws governing speech communication, i.e., the speech communication scientist?

2. What, if any, are the ethical responsibilities of the individual who applies this knowledge to practical communication decisions within the society, i.e., the speech communication practitioner?

Responsibilities of the scientist

The question of responsibility is not a new one; in fact, the physical sciences have been plagued by it for some time. When the physical sciences have produced the instruments for unlimited destruction as well as for unlimited progress, such concern is hardly surprising. More recently, however, the biological and, to a lesser extent, the behavioral sciences have been forced to consider the same problem. For example, the fields of genetics and biophysics are on the verge of discovering many of the basic secrets of human creation. Furthermore, in years to come, it will probably be possible to control systematically the kinds of human beings that are produced, to create a kind of hybrid species of Homo sapiens. The ethical ramifications of such discoveries are vividly clear. Should man tamper with the human reproductive processes in this manner? Or, consider a more specific question: Assume that the probability of an individual contracting cancer at some point in his life is .25, or one-fourth. By altering certain genetic combinations, this probability can be reduced to .01, or one-hundredth. There is, however, a problem. This particular change in genetic combinations increases the probability that the individual will become tubercular from .02, or two-hundredths, to .04, or four-hundredths. What are the ethical criteria for making the decision; or, in a broader context, is it ethical even to confront individuals with such decisions?[1]

When compared with issues such as these, the present ethical problems of speech communication may seem trivial. But it should be remembered that each new bit of knowledge increases the extent to which individuals can use speech communication to exercise behavioral control over others. Are such increases in control desirable? Should the quest for new information be terminated? If not, what are the ethical responsibilities of those who make this knowledge available?

Frequently, it has been argued that the scientist is free of any

---

[1] The noted biophysicist, Leroy Augenstein, has spoken extensively on this problem. The example employed is similar to one that he has utilized in his speeches.

ethical responsibility for his discoveries. For the speech communication scientist, this argument—let us call it the argument from scientific amorality—takes the following form: I am interested in the study of human behavior for its own sake, particularly those behaviors associated with the speech communication process. In my eyes, knowledge is a desirable end in itself, and I have no wish to apply this knowledge to practical problems. Certainly, others may use my discoveries for a host of purposes. They may employ my findings to increase the sale of aspirin or of skateboards, to develop in others more tolerant attitudes toward minority groups, to insure the election of a particular political candidate, or to convince the American public that an atomic attack should be launched on the Soviet Union. If people feel that certain of these objectives are unethical, they should not indict me. The parties who misapplied my discoveries are the real culprits.

Fortunately, it appears that most scientists find this argument increasingly dissatisfying; it has a sanctimonious ring, but it most certainly must result in psychological discomfort. After all, each of us participates in the adventure of human existence for twenty-four hours each day. Just as the businessman finds it difficult to adopt one code of ethics for the office and another for the rest of his daily transactions, so the scientist encounters obstacles when he attempts to place his roles as a scientist and as a concerned member of his society into separate psychological pigeonholes. To assert that, "As a citizen, I'm interested in preventing the exploitation of others by means of unethical speech communication, but as a scientist I'm not," is psychologically naive and intellectually pernicious.

Not only does this attitude of injured innocence generate an invidious, amoral climate, it may result in scientists who are astoundingly naive about the ramifications of their research activities. This was vividly demonstrated at a recent meeting in which several graduate students were reporting the results of a research project. Basically, the study dealt with political images; i.e., the student investigators had sought to identify the traits that voters find attractive in political candidates. During the question period that followed the report, the author posed this question to the students: "Has it occurred to you that an unscrupulous campaign manager, with the assistance of good public-relations personnel, could take the knowledge that you have gained from this study and frame a series of political communications that could result in the election of a dishonest candidate? If such an undesirable event did occur, how much of the responsibility would be yours?"

The predominant response was one of startled confusion. As several of the students later admitted, they had never really given any thought to such questions. Their chagrin reflected not disinterest, but plain ignorance. That intelligent individuals should be ignorant of such questions is certainly undesirable. Even if no two of these students could agree on the answer to the question, it seems essential that they be forced to come to grips with it.

If the doctrine of scientific amorality is not a satisfactory solution to the problem of responsibility, what other alternatives remain? Of course, one could argue that all research activity should be suspended, that the scientific quest for new knowledge should cease. Even if it were possible to enforce such a restriction, it would have deleterious effects. To renounce the value of knowledge, to become intellectual ostriches with heads buried in the sand: these are not worthy human actions. Rather, the speech communication scientist must continue to seek new knowledge, while remaining cognizant of the ethical responsibilities entailed by his search. How can this burden of responsibility best be borne? The following suggested answer to this question is both highly tentative and subject to change.

Start with the assumption, stated earlier in this volume, that attempts at manipulation and control have always been, and will continue to be, a vital thread in the fabric of human experience. Given this a priori starting point, the question of control versus no control becomes a dead issue. Rather, the issues of importance involve the ends sought by those who employ manipulation and control and the identification of those individuals who should exercise such control.

Fortunately, our political and social system permits each of us to voice our opinions and beliefs on these latter issues. By giving voice to his opinions, the speech communication scientist, in his capacity as a concerned and informed citizen, can demonstrate his concern for the ethical implications of his work. He can give public expression to those values judged desirable, and he can offer his professional services to those causes and individuals deemed worthy of support. He can promulgate the doctrine of ethical responsibility among his colleagues. In short, he can accept the premise that his existence as a scientist and his existence as a responsible human being are inseparable.

Some critics will scoff at this solution. They will assert that scientists, like all other citizens, suffer from a chronic failure to agree on value premises. But should we not encourage disagreement and controversy in preference to feigned indifference? Although it may be impossible to know the truth or falsity of value statements, decisions must be made. Because the speech communication scientist seeks to provide knowledge that may influence the course of such decisions, it is criminally remiss for him to remove himself from the arena of conflict. After all, honest disagreement, not detached withdrawal, is the bedrock of a democratic society.

It can also be argued that the very laws sought by the speech communication scientist can be employed in a manner calculated to destroy the democratic institutions to which we have just appealed. Certainly, one must grant this possibility; even so, vigilance and active participation by all interested citizens are the best means of preventing such a calamitous happening. In addition, such an argument can easily be reduced to an absurdity—knowledge from almost any field can be misapplied to bring about unjust political and social changes. And even if we put an end to all intellectual progress, what is currently known could be misapplied for the same undesirable purposes. After all, speech communication can be used as a tool **to preserve,** as well as **to destroy,** our societal foundations; and it is better that speech communication scientists continue to seek new knowledge, while attempting to insure that it be used for positive purposes.

A scientist's eventual commitment on the issue of responsibility must, of necessity, embrace numerous personal considerations. Certainly, the adherents of scientific amorality have constructed a logically tidy argument. For the author, however, some muddle-headed uncertainty is preferable to a psychologically indefensible position. To paraphrase the remarks of a most respected professor, some philosophies and viewpoints are silly, primarily because we know at the common-sense level that people do not behave that way.

Responsibilities of the practitioner

If anything, the state of ethical affairs in the crowded economic and social marketplace facetiously referred to as "the real world" is even more confused than in the academic confines of the speech communication scientist's laboratory. For in the "real world," knowledge about speech communication is no longer an end in itself; instead, its value is determined by the extent to which it can be successfully applied to the achievement of other ends: the sale of skateboards, the election of political candidates, the development of better public safety programs. What ethical restraints should be placed on individuals employing speech communication for these purposes? To what extent are these people ethically responsible for the consequences of their speech communication? These are indeed difficult questions to answer.

Once again, it can be argued that questions of morality are largely irrelevant. If I am assigned the task of writing radio commercials for a particular corporation, my primary goal is to increase the product sales of that corporation. Because any other considerations are secondary, I should employ all of the information and techniques at my disposal to serve my client. If I am the campaign manager for a senatorial candidate, his election is paramount, and I should leave no stone unturned in the quest for votes. If I am a fund raiser for a philanthropic organization, the success or failure of my campaign is judged solely by the number of dollars that I accumulate. In short, once the end has been defined, one should use any means available to achieve it.

In general, society rejects such an extreme viewpoint regarding the ethics of everyday communication. One cannot libel or slander a political opponent without being placed in legal jeopardy. False and misleading advertising is forbidden by law. A deliberate lie, a gross invasion of privacy, communications that stress the violent consequences of failure to comply: these and many other communication techniques are considered repugnant by most members of society.

But to combat all of these ethical violations, society has imposed a system of external controls. Certain situations are more subtle; they involve matters of internal restraints. For example, assume that you are the speech writer for a particular senatorial candidate. Although you are not completely certain, you suffer from nagging doubts concerning his honesty. Even so, you continue to compose his speeches, making use of data that indicate that the majority of voters like candidates who project an image of virility and manliness. You are successful in creating this image of your candidate, and he wins election handily. Midway through his term of office, a political scandal erupts, and it is discovered that the senator has been bilking his constituents out of money designated to the state in the form of federal grants. What, if any, responsibility should you assume for this unfortunate occurrence?

Your initial doubts concerning the honesty of your candidate should give you cause for ethical concern. To be sure, decisions must usually be made on the basis of probabilities; even so, the circumstances in this particular case suggest a need for further investigation of the candidate. You should struggle to determine whether or not you made every reasonable effort to insure yourself of the senator's integrity; and, if not, you should be willing to admit that you acted hastily in support of a poor cause.

This latter admission is extremely difficult, particularly as most individuals are seldom, if ever, willing to grant that the causes that they champion are questionable. This unwillingness stems not from dishonesty, but from psychological characteristics common to the human species. Usually, we feel psychologically uncomfortable if we are caught in the inconsistency of giving support to a cause that we consider unjust. As a result, where we continue to lend our efforts, we usually manage to convince ourselves of the sterling characteristics of our purpose.[2]

But to say that an admission of error is difficult is not to argue against its desirability. After all, the ability to impose internal restraints on oneself is an essential prerequisite for the maintenance of a democratic society. If the only controls imposed on speech communication are external ones, individual freedoms must suffer. Although the problem of ethical responsibility for speech communication practitioners is a thorny one, it cannot be avoided by an appeal to irrelevance. Instead, each of us, in his daily activities as a communicator, must strive conscientiously to evaluate the ethical merits of every course of action and to impose upon himself the internal restraints essential to the maintenance of a free society.

Summary

This chapter has briefly discussed two ethical questions of concern to students of speech communication: what, if any, are the ethical

---

[2]This desire for psychological consistency has been dealt with extensively by so-called balance, or consistency, theorists. For a summary of their position see Ivan Preston, "Inconsistency: A Persuasive Device" in **Dimensions in Communication,** eds. James H. Campbell and Hal W. Hepler (Belmont, California: Wadsworth, 1965), pp. 95–102.

responsibilities of speech communication scientists; and what, if any, are the ethical responsibilities of speech communication practitioners? It was suggested that ethical questions cannot be begged by an appeal to irrelevance; rather, the very nature of a democratic society requires acceptance of certain ethical responsibilities by scientist and practitioner alike. Although the nature and extent of such ethical commitments must, of necessity, remain a highly personal matter, it was stressed that internal restraints are an essential ingredient of the ethical practice of speech communication.

Selected bibliography

The selections in this bibliography are intended as a sampling of relevant material for the student of speech communication. Since a comprehensive bibliography is an impossibility, readings have been chosen because of their direct pertinence to the issues discussed in this volume, or because they focused on problems that are closely related to these issues. As would be expected, some selections are more demanding than others, and the reader will have to choose on the basis of his own background in the area.

Books

Berelson, Bernard, and Steiner, Gary A. **Human Behavior: An Inventory of Scientific Findings.** New York: Harcourt, Brace & World, 1964.

Berlo, David K. **The Process of Communication.** New York: Holt, Rinehart and Winston, 1960.

Bormann, Ernest G. **Theory and Research in the Communicative Arts.** New York: Holt, Rinehart and Winston, 1965.

Brehm, Jack W. and Cohen, Arthur R. **Explorations in Cognitive Dissonance.** New York: Wiley, 1962.

Brown, J. A. C. **Techniques of Persuasion: From Propaganda to Brainwashing.** Baltimore: Penguin, 1963.

Brown, Roger William. **Words and Things.** Glencoe: The Free Press, 1958.

Campbell, James H., and Hepler, Hal W., eds. **Dimensions in Communication.** Belmont, California: Wadsworth, 1965.

Cherry, Colin. **On Human Communication: A Review, a Survey, and a Criticism.** Cambridge, Massachusetts, and New York: The Technology Press of Massachusetts Institute of Technology and Wiley, 1957.

Cohen, Arthur R. **Attitude Change and Social Influence.** New York: Basic, 1964.

Eisenson, Jon, Auer, J. Jeffery, and Irwin, John V. **The Psychology of Communication.** New York: Appleton-Century-Crofts, 1963.

Hayakawa, S. I. **Language in Thought and Action.** 2nd ed. New York: Harcourt, Brace & World, 1964.

Hovland, Carl I., Janis, Irving L., and Kelley, Harold H. **Communication and Persuasion: Psychological Studies of Opinion Change.** New Haven: Yale University Press, 1953.

Kaplan, Abraham. **The Conduct of Inquiry: Methodology for Behavioral Science.** San Francisco: Chandler, 1964.

Schramm, Wilbur Lang, ed. **The Science of Human Communication: New Directions and New Findings in Communication Research.** New York: Basic, 1963.

Sherif, Carolyn W., Sherif, Muzafer, and Nebergall, Roger. **Attitude and Attitude Change: The Social Judgment–Involvement Approach.** Philadelphia: Saunders, 1965.

Skinner, B. F. **Verbal Behavior.** ("The Century Psychology Series.") New York: Appleton-Century-Crofts, 1957.

Weaver, Carl H., and Strausbaugh, Warren L. **Fundamentals of Speech Communication.** New York: American Book, 1964.

Articles

Becker, Samuel L. "Research on Emotional and Logical Proofs," **The Southern Speech Journal,** XXVIII (Spring 1963), 198–208.

Bettinghaus, Erwin P. "The Operation of Congruity in an Oral Communication Situation," **Speech Monographs,** XXVIII (August 1961), 131–142.

Deutsch, Karl W. "On Communication Models in the Social Sciences," **Public Opinion Quarterly,** XVI (Fall 1952), 356–380.

Diggs, B. J. "Persuasion and Ethics," **Quarterly Journal of Speech,** L (December 1964), 359–374.

Eubanks, Ralph T., and Baker, Virgil L. "Toward an Axiology of Rhetoric," **Quarterly Journal of Speech,** XLVIII (April 1962), 157–169.

Feather, N. T. "A Structural Balance Model of Communication Effects," **Psychological Review,** LXXI (July 1964), 291–314.

Gerbner, George. "Toward a General Model of Communication," **Audio-Visual Communication Review,** IV (Summer 1956), 171–199.

Johnson, F. Craig, and Klare, George R. "General Models of Communication Research: A Survey of the Developments of a Decade," **Journal of Communication,** XI (March 1961), 13–26 and 45.

Johnson, Wendell L. "The Spoken Word and the Great Unsaid," **Quarterly Journal of Speech,** XXXVII (December 1951), 419–430.

Kelman, Herbert C. "Compliance, Identification, and Internalization: Three Processes of Attitude Change," **Journal of Conflict Resolution,** II (March 1958), 51–60.

———. "Processes of Opinion Change," **Public Opinion Quarterly,** XXV (Spring 1961), 57–79.

Miller, Gerald R. "Theory in Quantitative Speech Research," **Western Speech,** XXVIII (Winter 1964), 15–22.

Newcomb, Theodore M. "An Approach to the Study of Communicative Acts," **Psychological Review,** LX (November 1953), 393–404.

Nilsen, Thomas R. "Free Speech, Persuasion, and the Democratic Process," **Quarterly Journal of Speech,** XLIV (October 1958), 235–244.

———. "On Defining Communication," **The Speech Teacher,** VI (January 1957), 10–18.

Thompson, Wayne N. "A Conservative View of a Progressive Rhetoric," **Quarterly Journal of Speech,** XLIX (February 1963), 1–8.

Wallace, Karl R. "The Substance of Rhetoric: Good Reasons," **Quarterly Journal of Speech,** XLIX (October 1963), 239–250.

Westley, Bruce H., and MacLean, Malcolm S., Jr. "A Conceptual Model for Communication Research," **Journalism Quarterly,** XXXIV (Winter 1957), 31–38.

Index of names

Subject index